ON THE IGNATIAN WAY

JOSÉ LUIS IRIBERRI, S.J.
CHRIS LOWNEY

On the Ignatian Way

~

*A Pilgrimage in the Footsteps
of Saint Ignatius of Loyola*

TRANSLATED BY
CHRISTOPHER J. LOCASCIO

IGNATIUS PRESS   SAN FRANCISCO

Original Spanish edition:
El Camino Ignaciano
Un camino de sanación hacia la libertad
© 2015 by Ediciones Mensajero, Bilbao

Cover design by Enrique J. Aguilar

© 2018 by Ignatius Press, San Francisco
All rights reserved
ISBN 978-1-62164-146-9
Library of Congress Control Number 2017932734
Printed in the United States of America ∞

Contents

III. PRAYING THE IGNATIAN WAY:
A DAILY GUIDE
by *Chris Lowney*

Contents

Preface

We present this guide, written collaboratively by various European, Australian, and North American authors, in order to offer pilgrims an instrument that might help them to advance on their interior way. All the authors are themselves experienced pilgrims, not only on the Ignatian Way, but also on other pilgrimages. It is on the basis of their own experience and knowledge of Ignatian spirituality that they propose this interior guide. The first and second parts are descriptive of the pilgrims' own experience, as testimony of what can happen. The third part is devoted to an adaptation of the *Spiritual Exercises* specific to the Ignatian pilgrimage. José Luis Iriberri, S.J., was the final editor of the work, but he has respected as much as possible the original styles of each author.

The Ignatian Way:
A New Pilgrimage for a New Age

by José Luis Iriberri, S.J.

We begin here a journey following the trails of the Ignatian Way from Loyola to Manresa and Barcelona. Every pilgrimage route is born from the initiative of someone, in this case, the Society of Jesus; an initiative confirmed in the commission the provincial superiors have given to me and my two companions in adventure, Jaime Badiola, S.J., and Chris Lowney. At the end of 2010, we began to design this new pilgrimage for the twenty-first century following the footsteps of Saint Ignatius, our holy founder. Clearly, the goal we set before ourselves was apostolic, linked from its beginning to the experience of the *Spiritual Exercises*. We understood that a way of pilgrimage always had to be an instrument at the service of the human person, of his growth as a person for the sake of some ideals, constantly responding to the inner search for meaning and happiness. It was in this way that the "Ignatian Way" was born, accompanied and assisted by more than thirty volunteers from five different countries, all of them connected to the spirit and legacy of Ignatius.

This is the formal beginning, but in reality a true Way of Pilgrimage is created through the hundreds and thousands of experiences that pilgrims have had throughout the years.

The pilgrimage is created by the pilgrims and by the interaction that is established between their experience and the inhabitants of each town and city they encounter along their path. As has been studied and well said, with the passage of pilgrims, territories are united, habits are changed, and new cultures are even created, thanks to the dialogues, the laughter, and the exchange of knowledge that is produced in the paths trodden by the sandals or boots of the pilgrims. It would be unfair not to recognize the transfer of knowledge in health, cuisine, and architecture, among many others, that came to medieval Europe from the Iberian Peninsula thanks, for example, to the Way of Saint James (Camino de Santiago): the pilgrims, some rich and others poor, some nobles and others plebian, explained and shared not only their spiritual experiences but also the novelties that were produced in such disparate cultures as those through which they traveled.

This humble text attempts to initiate that tradition which would construct the Ignatian Way based on the pilgrims, its true champions. A particular experience says very little; therefore, rather than relate my own experience, I unite with those of other pilgrims to construct our account together. It is none other than this which is the spirit of pilgrimage: to create profound and transforming communion with God. It is our sincere wish that the nearly 435 miles of the Ignatian Way may serve also today to unite people from many cultures and with different interests.

My own experience as a pilgrim now amounts to some thousands of miles, mostly alone and on foot, as the master Ignatius of Loyola often proposed. But if, upon speaking of pilgrimages, the reader is left with the impression that the important thing is the distance or the miles covered, he would be making a mistake in his approach that I would like to help to clear up: to go on pilgrimage is not to walk the maximum number of miles in the minimum amount of time. This would be a physical competition or, if you like, a spiritual voyage in which the physical component is the most important, which would put the body before the spirit. Those who know the ways of pilgrimage know very well that, the more space the physical body occupies, the less personal time and space is left for the spiritual dimension. The "external physical way" is no more than a precious instrument to open the door to the "interior way", which leads the pilgrim to discover himself as a profound being and, from our Ignatian viewpoint, as a being profoundly loved by the One who gives origin to the universe and who gives life to each of us individually. And to come to this, to feel deeply loved, the person does not need to walk thousands of miles, not even a few hundred: the *God who surprises us* and who surprised Ignatius in his room at Loyola also awaits us at whatever point of the journey we follow. Paraphrasing the master, we know that it is not many miles that fill and satisfy the soul, but savoring inwardly that which we experience in each step.

One of the pilgrims who collaborated in the writing of these pages that we present, Sarah Davies, after her thirty days of pilgrimage, shares with us this anecdote:

> On the way home, on the first leg of the plane trip I sat beside a man who had been touring Europe, ending up in Spain. Among other things, he asked me about what I had been doing; and when I told him about my Ignatian pilgrimage, his first question was about how many miles I had walked. Only 250? Well . . . that is not bad, but he had a friend who had walked 500 miles on the Way of Saint James. His reaction made me think. If people think that a pilgrimage is a competition of miles, it would be good if

in these pages we show a different side of what a pilgrim-age is.

It seems to me very pertinent to begin with this commentary, since it touches on the essence of what we want to contribute with our reflection: a pilgrimage like ours is measured, not by the distance or the speed, but by the depth at which we arrive, entering into contact with our inner selves and with that God who lives within us. And this encounter is achieved by walking, certainly, and also through the human relationships, the meditation, the contemplation of the surroundings, the effort, the conversations, the lessons learned about one's own life, and the new meanings that appear in it.

Throughout these brief pages, we are going to travel together this journey which is the Ignatian Way, trying to communicate feelings and ideas through our interwoven experiences as pilgrims on the same path.

Let us get started, then, and Buen Camino!

I

WALKING WITH IGNATIUS

by Chris Lowney

I

Make the Way by Walking It

Caminante, no hay camino. Se hace camino al andar.
(Traveler, there is no way. The way is made by
walking it.)
                              —Antonio Machado, d. 1939

Do not be frightened, aspiring pilgrim; you do not have
to take the poet Antonio Machado *too* literally. There *is* a
way from Loyola to Manresa along the route that Ignatius
of Loyola followed in 1522, and this book describes it in
detail.

But the evocative verse by Machado captures an important truth: make *your own* Way. It is true that you are going
to follow in the footsteps of Ignatius, but let it be your own
desires, hopes, and worries—personal and untransferable—
that push you forward.

After all, that is exactly what Ignatius did: he also followed the footsteps of others (for hundreds of years before he set out, many people had already gone on pilgrimage to Montserrat to venerate the famous Black Madonna,
the *Moreneta*). But it was his search for God and questions
about life that impelled him. And whatever ideas came to
his mind along the path were uniquely his own. It will happen again with you. Let this book guide your steps on the
path of Ignatius from Loyola to Manresa, but allow it to

be your own ideas and prayers that guide your heart. Keep in mind the reminder of the poet Machado: it is you who make your own way on the pilgrimage and in life. The way holds something in store exclusively for you! Following the route of Ignatius through Spain, find yourself and find your own path in life.

Recreate the journey that changed history

The pilgrimage of Ignatius of Loyola changed his life and changed history; modern pilgrims will enjoy the privilege of recreating one of the most important journeys on foot in the history of mankind.

We will outline the biography of Ignatius later; in the following paragraphs, we will try to justify the seemingly extravagant statement: the journey on foot of Ignatius "changed history". Did it really?

Yes, without a doubt.

This Ignatian pilgrimage began (as does this book) in the home of Ignatius in Loyola and ended in Manresa (near Barcelona), where he was graced with a profound spiritual illumination. At a later time in his life, Ignatius evaluated his pilgrim phase and made it clear how profoundly he was marked by one of the experiences he had in Manresa: "If he were to gather all the helps he received from God and everything he knew, and add them together, he does not think they would add up to all that he received on that one occasion" (*PJ*, p. 79).[1]

---

[1] All quotations from the autobiography of Saint Ignatius have been taken from *A Pilgrim's Journey: The Autobiography of Ignatius of Loyola*, rev. ed., trans. Joseph N. Tylenda, S.J. (San Francisco: Ignatius Press, 2001; abbreviated hereafter as *PJ*).

Fortunately for us, Ignatius did not keep for himself the ideas he had in Manresa. During his pilgrimage, he jotted down verses from Scripture and various thoughts, but also the rudiments of the *Spiritual Exercises*, meditations that guide those who undertake them to consider the miracle implied by the fact of having been created, the love that God has for them, and the reality of sin; the exercitants reflect on the life of Jesus and on how to follow him in the specific circumstances of their lives.

It required of Ignatius much effort to arrive at a new understanding of himself; he had to go through personal trauma, a pilgrimage, and a profound conversion, as well as great suffering and great joys. His genius was in translating his own journey toward illumination into a series of exercises that any one of us can perform.

The *Exercises* developed in Manresa are the "number one proof" in our argument that the pilgrimage of Ignatius changed history, because these *Exercises* have touched millions and millions of people. At present, hundreds of centers of spirituality and retreat houses offer adaptations of them every year, from Massachusetts to India and anywhere in between. At this very moment, the cloister of a university in the Philippines might be discussing ideas arising from these *Exercises*, perhaps an executive has entered an on-line forum on the *Exercises* before going to work, and it is possible that a group of high school students is participating in a day retreat based on the text of Ignatius. (Part 3 of this book invites you to carry out your own daily adaptation of these *Spiritual Exercises*.)

But the *Exercises* are not the only fruit of Ignatius' pilgrimage that changed the world: his journey on foot was the first step toward the founding of the Society of Jesus,

better known as the Jesuits. In the course of their long and
unlikely history, the Jesuits helped to invent the Vietnamese
alphabet, founded one of the largest cities in the world (São
Paulo), and negotiated the border treaty between Russia and
China. Currently, nearly five centuries after their founding,
some nineteen thousand Jesuits work shoulder to shoulder
with a several times larger number of laity, active in more
than a hundred countries. Together they manage the largest
private network of higher education in the whole world, ed-
ucate yearly a million students in the poorest neighborhoods
of Latin America, accompany around a million refugees
displaced by war or hunger, and serve in parishes, retreat
houses, and many other institutions.

It is true that it was not during his pilgrimage that Ignatius
decided to found a religious order of many members and
great prestige; but the experience that he had in the course of
it oriented him toward a new focus when it came to seeking
his place in the world. And this new way of thinking led,
some years later, to the founding of the Jesuits. For Ignatius
realized something fundamental: Christian life is not about
mimicking or outdoing the saints (or any other people), but
about living one's own life putting personal talents and gifts
at the service of God's plan for mankind. God inspired Francis of Assisi to do what he could do: the sanctity of Francis
blossomed when he wed his particular gifts with the needs
of his time.

You and I (and Ignatius) each have different gifts, and we
live in unique circumstances. Perhaps Saint Francis and Saint
Teresa inspire us by their courage, holiness, and determination. But, once inspired by them, we must discover how to
put into practice our own unique talents in the particular
circumstances in which we live. (And indeed, traversing the

Ignatian Way offers you a magnificent opportunity to reflect on *your* own talents and the best way to utilize them.)

Ignatius and his first companions, among them Francis Xavier, took refuge in this wisdom when, in time, they decided to found the Jesuits, whose spirituality, formation, and worldview were (and since then always have been) fundamentally dominated by the methods and ideals of the *Spiritual Exercises*. Consider the influence of these *Spiritual Exercises* and the achievements of Jesuits and associated laity throughout five centuries: without doubt, the man who left Loyola with a mule and few personal belongings has much to show us about the time he spent on the way. That journey on foot changed his story as well as the history of the world.

But equally important for the opportunity to recreate this history-making journey on foot will be your human relationship with its protagonist, Ignatius. The Ignatian Way offers the rare and maybe exclusive privilege of going on pilgrimage—metaphorically and spiritually—by the side of a saint.

Does this make any difference? Of course it does! Listen to what someone who has made the Ignatian Way says. The Irish Jesuit Terry Howard sums up the experience in the following way: "No amount of information or reading can replace the bare experience of following the footsteps of Ignatius, alone and on foot. I deepened my comprehension of Ignatius. I felt, in fact, that I walked beside him, seeing the landscapes and the views that he saw, walking the same route that he followed; and that I was able to explain to him how things looked today, as if I were his eyes fixed on a memory of his past."

Take full advantage of this opportunity. Discover your own twenty-first-century route, but travel together in your imagination with your companion of the sixteenth century. The pilgrimage of Ignatius changed the world; yours will, too, to a greater or lesser extent. His pilgrimage helped him to understand God's plan for him in a much deeper way and to shape the future direction of his life, and the same will happen to you.

2

Ignatius of Loyola:
The History of the Pilgrim

No modern person will identify with the circumstances of Ignatius of Loyola: after all, this was a nobleman, and he was caught up in swordsmanship and the conventions of medieval knighthood.

But we can all feel attracted to his story because most of us have experienced one version of it or another: his early plans and dreams were frustrated; obliged to reconsider who he was and where his life was headed, he undertook a voyage of reinvention. Gradually, he gained greater certainty about who he was as a person and what was important to him; but for a long time he did not know very well where the journey of his life was taking him. Sound familiar? Read now how Ignatius' history unfolded, and, as you do, draw from it ideas and perspectives for your own life journey.

Ignatius was born—probably in 1491—in the bosom of a family of the lower nobility of the Spanish Basque Country. Only some 10 percent of Spaniards could claim to be of noble lineage; but do not imagine a coddled Ignatius enjoying the luxury of a richly adorned castle while he waited to inherit an enormous fortune. Some branches of the Spanish

elite boasted dazzling riches, but the Loyola family, although
very comfortable, was not basking in wealth.

Additionally, Ignatius was the youngest of thirteen sib-
lings; whatever inheritance might accrue to him would be
more of a trickle than a flood. It is not surprising that two of
his brothers ended up seeking their fortune far from home
(one in Italy, and the other in the recently conquered Amer-
icas).

Neither did the young Ignatius, or Iñigo, as he was then
called, have a pampered and spoiled infancy. His father died
when he was fifteen years old; and his mother even earlier,
though historians do not know exactly when. In his letters,
Ignatius hardly mentions her, which is why historians sup-
pose that she must have died while he was still very young.
It is likely that the wife of the town blacksmith, his wet
nurse, became a kind of mother for him.

We do not know much, because Ignatius tells us little.
In the 130 pages that comprise his autobiography, he dedi-
cates only one sentence to his life before reaching the age
of twenty-six: "Up to his twenty-sixth year he was a man
given to worldly vanities, and having a vain and overpow-
ering desire to gain renown, he found special delight in the
exercise of arms" (*PJ*, p. 37).

Though he could not leave him any riches or even a sensi-
ble way of life, Ignatius' father turned to family relations in
order to start looking for prestige for Ignatius. The treasurer
of the kingdom of Castile, related by marriage to the Loy-
olas, accepted Ignatius as a page. When he was about fifteen,
Ignatius was sent to live in the home of this court official
in Arévalo, some 185 miles from his birthplace. He lived
comfortably, learned the protocols of life at court, learned
how to handle a sword and other weapons, and had the
chance to eavesdrop on meetings between the most distin-

guished personalities of Spain: King Ferdinand, for example, who with his wife, Isabella, had financed the expeditions of Christopher Columbus, visited Arévalo several times while Ignatius resided there.

Ignatius was also a troublemaker. It seems that he had an impetuous nature; following a scuffle in a narrow alley, for example, he drew his sword and chased his opponents down the street. One of his Jesuit confidants years later described the young Iñigo as "especially disordered in what had to do with gambling, affairs with women, and duels". On one occasion, he was arrested for what the judicial records called "enormous and premeditated crimes". Though the tale sounds intriguing, the documents do not offer additional details. But, however execrable the crime may have been, well-connected people—then as now—are not always subject to the same norms as other mortals. Ignatius remained free and without charges, and the prestige that he so longed for continued to be within his reach.

Until, suddenly, it was not. Ignatius tasted the bitter truth that was sung in the coronation ceremonies of the popes in days gone by: *sic transit gloria mundi*, or, loosely translated, earthly glory is ephemeral. While Ignatius was still in his twenties, King Ferdinand died, and the new king transferred the privileges and properties of the royal treasurer to Ferdinand's widow. Thus, young Iñigo's patron was, in essence, evicted from his castle, and a large part of his wealth evaporated. With the prospects of his own family ruined, taking care of Ignatius could hardly be the main priority of the toppled royal treasurer. Nevertheless, he did what he could, for he let Ignatius go with two horses, a tidy sum of money, and a letter of introduction to the Duke of Nájera, another relative of the Loyola family.

But misfortune was to play a cruel trick on Ignatius again.

In fact, this seems to be the norm for the first part of his life, does it not? Well, in reality this is something that shapes most people's lives: paraphrasing Ecclesiastes, fortune or misfortune intervenes in the lives of each one of us. Some get bitter and throw in the towel when events do not live up to their expectations. Others learn to accept setbacks and persevere. Take the case of Ignatius: he had been born into a noble family, but too late—a dozen children too late—to have the right to a good inheritance. He had been the page of an illustrious and powerful royal treasurer, but the influence of his protector soon waned, before Ignatius was able to get established. After that, Ignatius secured a position with the Duke of Nájera, but the dominions of the duke would soon erupt into a chaos that would transform the life of Ignatius forever.

Oversimplifying a somewhat complex background, Spain, as we know it today, was being forged in the decades before Ignatius was born and during the course of his life. The Iberian Peninsula had for a long time been divided into a mosaic of kingdoms. The Muslims had invaded the south of the peninsula from Northern Africa in 711, achieving dominion over it; Christian princes governed kingdoms situated in the north and the east of the peninsula, such as Castile, Aragon, Navarre, and Galicia. Little by little, the Christian kingdoms took back the territories ruled by the Muslims, and, toward the end of the fifteenth century, the consolidation of Spain accelerated. Queen Isabella of Castile and León contracted marriage with King Ferdinand of Aragon, merging their great kingdoms; in 1492, both conquered the last Muslim kingdom (Granada); and in 1512, Ferdinand took possession of Navarre, a small kingdom that for a long time had clung to its independence with respect to the neighboring French and Spanish kingdoms.

The Duke of Nájera, Iñigo's new protector, was named

viceroy of the recently conquered Navarre, and it is easy to imagine the tensions that he inherited. The Navarrese were furious about the loss of their independence. The fact that the ever more assertive Spaniards had expanded their dominion worried France, Spain's neighbor.

Thus, the French and some disaffected Navarrese saw that it was in their interest to ally in order to stir up trouble jointly. In 1521, some ten thousand French soldiers invaded Navarre, and some Navarrese united with them, offering loyalty to the invaders in exchange for the French promise to restore the rights and privileges they had recently lost at the hands of the Spaniards. The Spanish defenders, short on manpower, took shelter in the unfinished fortress of Pamplona; the Duke of Nájera turned and fled, leaving the fight for another day. His deputy then followed suit, taking hundreds of soldiers with him.

Ignatius stood his ground. Courage and honor won out over common sense. Ignatius describes the scene in his autobiography: "While everyone else clearly saw that they could not defend themselves and thought that they should surrender to save their lives, he offered so many reasons to the fortress' commander that he talked him into defending it. Though this was contrary to the opinion of all the other knights, still each drew encouragement from his firmness and fearlessness" (*PJ*, pp. 37–38).

The battle was over as soon as the cannonballs began to rain over the defenders of the fortress, who rapidly reconsidered the decision to fight and surrendered. But the surrender came one cannonball too late for Ignatius, who in his autobiography recalls that "a cannonball hit him in a leg, shattering it completely, and since the ball passed between both legs the other one was likewise severely wounded" (*PJ*, p. 39).

That did not mean the end of his life, but only the end

of the life that he had known until then. Not only was his leg broken; his plans for the future were also left shattered.

The pilgrim

He was taken home on a cot or stretcher; imagine the painful trip of more or less sixty miles on rough and uneven trails. The pain increased when, once in his hometown, the doctors, as Ignatius narrates in his autobiography, "agreed that the leg should be broken again and the bones reset, since they either had been poorly set in the first place or had become dislocated during the journey, for they were now out of joint and would never heal" (*PJ*, pp. 40–41). So, the fractured bones, which had been fusing already for some weeks, were again broken and reset (in an age when anesthesia did not exist!). Soon he began to manifest the "usual signs indicating the approach of death" (*PJ*, p. 41), because of which he was advised to confess and to receive the last rites.

Ignatius survived, but the restructured leg still did not heal adequately. Some bones in it overlapped others, making it shorter than the other, and it was also disfigured by an unsightly bulge. Ignatius probably imagined himself limping through the courtly galas with a bump stretching his tight leggings unaesthetically, and such an image terrified him even more than a new wrinkle on the face can afflict a vain celebrity of the twenty-first century. But the only solution was much more drastic than a quick Botox injection: Ignatius asked the surgeons if it was possible to cut off the piece of bone that stuck out. The idea horrified his family. Imagine the barbarity of such a surgical operation with a sixteenth century saw. Even so, despite the protests of his family, Ignatius "was determined to endure this martyrdom to satisfy his personal taste" (*PJ*, pp. 42–43).

Incredibly, he survived the operation. The recovery was slow, and Ignatius remained prostrate in bed for several weeks while the wounds healed. Time passed very slowly. Ignatius read everything he found at hand, which, without doubt, could not have been much in an age when printed books were scarce and costly. The library of his sister-in-law included little more than a life of Christ and a collection of biographies of saints.

He daydreamed constantly. He fantasized about the knightly feats that had for so long dominated his ambitions. But he also started to fantasize about pious plans to surpass the saints about whom he was reading: "What if I were to do what Saint Francis did, or to do what Saint Dominic did?" (*PJ*, p. 47). But something deeper than mere fantasy was unfolding. Two paths of life were vying for his loyalty: Would he go on preoccupied with worldly success, or was he going to serve God as the famous saints had?

Little by little, the desire to serve God began to prevail: "The greatest consolation he received at this time was from gazing at the sky and stars," Ignatius relates, "and this he often did and for quite a long time. The result of all this was that he felt within himself a strong impulse to serve our Lord" (*PJ*, pp. 50–51). The Latin roots of the term "conversion" imply a reorientation, and Ignatius was experiencing a slow but complete reorientation from one life-style to another. Beliefs that in his day he had pronounced merely with his lips in church were taking over his heart. While he was bedridden in the castle of Loyola, on occasion he suffered, feeling "a loathsomeness for all of his past life" (*PJ*,

p. 49), and he imagined the disciplines, abstinences, and other such exploits that "any generous soul on fire with God is accustomed to do" (*PJ*, p. 49).

Disgust for *all* of his past life? This statement will bother many readers, and it is good that it does so. Certainly, Ignatius had reasons to lament his past as a seducer and a tempestuous and self-obsessed person, just as many of us repent the missteps we have taken before the conversion of our lives to a healthier direction.

But Ignatius had also shown great virtues: loyalty, heroism, and courage. As happens with all people, his past included moments to be repented and moments to remember with gratitude. Nevertheless, Iñigo still was not capable of a careful examination of his life. His leg was healing, but his mind continued to be wounded. Plainly put (and with all due respect to this great saint), he seemed a bit crazy; the dangerous missile was aimed in the right direction, but the shot was prone to go astray. He still had not achieved the balance that he would later recommend to others: "Better great prudence and ordinary holiness than great holiness and little prudence."

Thus, with great holiness, but without much prudent planning, Ignatius decided that "his greatest desire, after regaining his health, was to go to Jerusalem" (*PJ*, p. 49) to visit the places where Jesus had lived and to imitate the abstinences and rigors of the great saints. We do not know if Ignatius explained all his plans to his family, but they heard enough to think that he was not in his right mind. His older brother "led him from room to room and with much love for him pleaded with him not to throw his life away" (*PJ*, p. 53). It is possible to imagine a twenty-first-century version of his brother's supplications: "You are obsessed with these crazy fantasies because of the great trauma that you suffered. Our family is still well-connected and can help you restart your career. But you are not young anymore; a dangerous and prolonged pilgrimage could completely ruin your already not very promising future."

On the Way

The family's protests were in vain. Ignatius' ambitions might have changed, but he went on being the same stubborn and brave person who had defended Pamplona when everyone else was inclined to surrender. Nothing was going to dissuade him from carrying out his pilgrimage. With the leg now well enough, he was anxious to begin his quest.

Ignatius did not leave a detailed chronology of his pilgrimage, but we can reconstruct its general phases. The recovery lasted some seven months. He began the pilgrimage sometime between the middle of January and the middle of February of 1522. He arrived at Montserrat on March 21 after having covered almost four hundred miles. On March 25, he left Montserrat to make a brief stop in the nearby locality of Manresa: a "brief stop" that would end up lasting almost a year.

What happened along the way? Ignatius tells us little in this regard. Surely there was an emotional farewell in the tower house of Loyola, but the sparse account of Ignatius does not reveal any sentimentality at all. He says only: "As he mounted his mule, another brother of his wanted to travel with him as far as Oñate", where one of their sisters lived. He spent a night at the famous sanctuary of Our Lady of Arantzazu, and there "that night he prayed for additional

strength for his journey" (*PJ*, p. 54). Years later, Ignatius
recalled this nocturnal vigil as a moment of greatest importance: "When God Our Lord showed me the mercy for me
to be able to change my life, I remember having received in
myself some benefit keeping vigil in the nave of the church
that night."

Ignatius and his brother separated in Oñate, and Ignatius
continued on to Navarrete, where the Duke of Nájera, his
former patron, resided. There he demanded that he be paid
what was owed him. Ignatius informs us that the Duke
"wanted to offer him . . . a position of authority, if he would
accept it" (*PJ*, p. 55). It is possible that the Duke remembered Iñigo's heroism in Pamplona as well as his own pre-
mature and unseemly flight.

But Ignatius, fully committed to his new life and to the
pilgrimage with which he was starting it, was hardly going
to let himself be deterred from his plans by a job offer. He
refused the proposal, collected the money that was owed to
him, ordered that a part of it be distributed "among certain
individuals to whom he felt some obligation" (ibid.), allo-
cated the rest for the repair of one of his favorite images
of the Virgin Mary, dismissed the two servants who had
accompanied him from Loyola, and "departed Navarrete,
and, riding his mule, he headed for Montserrat" (*PJ*, p. 56).

From there, the trip appears to have lasted some three
weeks, and although Ignatius did not record the journey
that he followed day by day, we can be fairly sure of the
route that he took. After all, long-distance travelers had few
options at the time, and the regular approach was to stick to
the routes laid out centuries before, when Spain formed part
of the extensive Roman Empire. The important Roman city
of Cesaraugusta, the modern-day Saragossa, had been connected with the Mediterranean coast by a road that followed

the path of the Ebro River; and the excellently constructed Roman roads continued to exist long after the fall of the Roman Empire, the basis of the medieval "royal highways" that Ignatius traveled, well-established routes on which travelers knew that they could find lodging and supplies every few miles. Ignatius had no reason to improvise and forge his own way to Montserrat. (The present-day Ignatian Way likewise follows the medieval route, though it does not always recreate the exact path of Ignatius: the modern Spanish freeways have replaced some stretches of the medieval route, and for this reason walking where Ignatius walked would mean dodging the high-speed traffic of the freeways. It is not recommended.)

Ignatius offers hardly any details of what he did and thought along the way. It is evident that he mortified himself with severe abstinence and fasting and with what he calls "great penances". Reflecting upon those days as a pilgrim, as he dictated years later his autobiography, Ignatius confesses that at that time his soul was "still blind" (*PJ*, p. 56). That is, he was burning with desire to serve God, but he strove to do it by merely imitating and trying to surpass the saints about whom he had read so much. That is what he focused on; "he never considered anything about the interior life, nor did he know what humility was, or charity, or patience, or that discretion was the rule and measure of these virtues" (*PJ*, pp. 56–57). The Greek philosopher Aristotle wrote of justice, wisdom, courage, and moderation as the four great human virtues, which balance one another. To use Aristotle's barometer, Ignatius was courageous beyond all measure, was growing in wisdom, lacked moderation altogether, and, as a consequence, was at times confused about what had to do with justice, as another incident that took place during the long walk clearly manifests.

Ignatius mentions that he encountered a Muslim on the way. Keep in mind that Arab and North African Muslims invaded Spain in 711 and dominated the Iberian Peninsula for hundreds of years. Although Ferdinand and Isabella had reconquered the last Muslim kingdom (Granada) in 1492 and, a decade later, the majority of Muslims had been required to convert to Christianity or to emigrate, in Aragon a decree of expulsion had not yet been promulgated, in part because the Muslim craftsmen and peasants of this Christian kingdom contributed to the economy in an important way. Ignatius was walking toward a new life, and the same was true, sadly, for this Muslim, who three years later would have to face the devastating dilemma of abandoning his homeland or renouncing his religion.

Ignatius tells us that "in their conversation they began to speak about our Lady" (*PJ*, p. 57). Such a topic of conversation may surprise Christian readers, but Mary is, in fact, profoundly venerated by Muslims; for example, in the Qur'an she is mentioned even more frequently than in the New Testament. Maybe Ignatius was pleasantly surprised to hear this person speak affectionately of Mary, but Christian and Muslim beliefs about Mary ultimately differ, and Ignatius became aggressive when the Muslim confessed that "he could not believe that in giving birth she remained a virgin" (ibid.).

The conversation ended on that bad note, and when the Muslim went ahead on his mule, Ignatius was left brooding bitterly and became incensed; nobles should defend the honor of the ladies, and he had not defended the honor of the purest of ladies in the face of the Muslim blasphemy. He began to plot vengeance with the same impetuous fury that had inflamed his past street scuffles: "He now desired to search out the Moor and strike him with his dagger for all that he had said" (*PJ*, p. 58).

But Ignatius was unable to decide. Was stabbing another person behavior worthy of a Christian? With his thoughts whirling in a confusing alternation between vengeance and piety, to the rhythm of the mule's steps, Ignatius ended up resolving, as incredible as it seems, to let the mule decide. The *mule*? When they neared a fork in the road, perhaps between Luceni and Pedrola (Ignatius does not say, but there are historians who point to this place), he loosened the reins with the idea that "if the mule took the road to the village, he would then search out the Moor and use his dagger on him" (*PJ*, pp. 58–59). On the other hand, if the mule continued on the main road, Ignatius would leave the Moor alone. The pious Ignatius did nothing other than to put the mule's reins in God's hands.

It is possible that God took the reins. Whether by divine intervention or by the same blind luck of a coin tossed in the air, the mule did not go after the Moor but followed the royal highway, to the good fortune of the Moor, Ignatius, and all those who in the following five centuries have benefited from Jesuit education or spirituality. (A Jesuit who was not very knowledgeable about horses once told me this story, adding at the end the following witticism: "And that was the first but not the last time that a critical decision in the Society of Jesus was made by an ass.")

The autobiography of Ignatius relates only one other episode of the weeks prior to his arrival at Montserrat. He stopped in a large town (maybe Igualada) to buy proper pilgrim attire: "He bought some sackcloth—it was of a loose weave and bristly to the touch" (*PJ*, p. 59), with which to make himself a tunic. He also acquired a walking stick, or pilgrim's staff, and a small drinking gourd, the traditional equipment of medieval pilgrims.

Once he had crossed the flat and occasionally desert-like Aragon countryside, the sight of a considerably different landscape told him that he was now approaching the monastery of Our Lady of Montserrat, the principal stop on the Spanish leg of his pilgrimage. The word Montserrat itself—a Catalan term that means "serrated mountain"—helps us to imagine the lame Ignatius, exhausted from the trip, toiling in the climb of about 4250 feet through rugged and rocky terrain up to the monastic complex that had been attracting pilgrims since the ninth century.

The unique peaks of Montserrat appear almost otherworldly, and the panoramic views are spectacular. But the determined Ignatius mentions nothing of this. Instead, he writes that he dedicated three full days to the composition of a general confession of all the sins of his life. Three days? Could even the most immoral of reprobates have committed such an abundant catalogue of sins that he needed three whole days to commit them to writing? Probably not. Ignatius was showing the signs of the unhealthy scruples that would haunt him until his spirituality matured still more in Manresa.

Once this confession was completed, Ignatius entrusted his sword and dagger to the monastery to be hung as an offering next to the famous image of the Black Virgin, or *Moreneta* (a replica of the sword is still there; the original is in the Jesuit church of Barcelona). Then he donned his crude pilgrim's garb and gave the higher-quality clothing of his past life to a beggar. Ignatius was shedding the showiness of the worldly knight and had decided to "clothe himself in the livery of Christ" (*PJ*, p. 61).

Wrapped in the sackcloth, Ignatius "went to kneel before our Lady's altar. He spent the entire night there, sometimes on his knees, sometimes standing erect, with his pilgrim's staff in hand" (*PJ*, p. 62).

He left Montserrat the next morning in the direction of the port city of Barcelona, where he could embark to Rome, to direct his course from there to Venice, the port from which pilgrim ships set sail in the direction of the Holy Land. But he did not take the direct road from Montserrat to Barcelona, afraid to run across "many who knew and respected him" (ibid.). He was a penitent covered with sackcloth and did not want to run into well-positioned families known from his former life, for fear that they might invite him to join up with a comfortable entourage. So, on secondary roads, he diverted to the small locality of Manresa with the intention to "remain for several days in a hospital and jot down a few items in the book" (*PJ*, p. 63), that is, in the diary that he was conscientiously keeping "and that afforded him much consolation" (ibid.).

It just so happened that a woman called Inés Pascual was traveling the same way, and this woman later described her first impressions of Ignatius: "He was not very tall; his skin was pale and the color of rose flesh; he had a handsome and serious face; . . . he was very tired and limped with his right leg." She and her traveling companions offered to take Ignatius to the local hospice, but they constantly found themselves obliged to slacken their pace due to Ignatius "because it hurt him to walk".

The few days that he had planned to spend in Manresa stretched out into eleven extraordinarily important months. Consider only one indication among many possible others: Ignatius spent 2 percent of his life in Manresa; nevertheless, this period takes up 25 percent of his autobiography. There, profoundly moving mystical visions came to him unexpectedly, which he would later struggle to express in words. One day, for example, "it was granted him to understand, with great spiritual joy, the way in which God had created the world. He seemed to see a white object with rays stemming from it, from which God made light. He neither knew how to explain these things nor did he fully remember the spiritual lights that God had then imprinted on his soul" (*PJ*, p. 76). At the time when he tries to help us comprehend the content of his visions, Ignatius makes their impact unmistakably clear: "One day . . . his understanding was raised on high, so as to see the Most Holy Trinity under the aspect of three keys on a musical instrument, and as a result he shed many tears and sobbed so strongly that he could not control himself" (*PJ*, p. 75).

Manresa continues to be the beloved Jesuit archetype of spiritual illumination: dozens and dozens of Jesuit retreat houses and spiritual centers around the world bear the name of this city. Nevertheless, the Cardoner River, beside which Ignatius enjoyed such profound illumination, is nothing special; it is no more seductive than countless rivers that run through countless cities. And that is just the point: it is not necessary to travel to Manresa to draw near to God. For that, one can go anyplace, or no place at all. Montserrat and Manresa are not spiritual lollipops at the end of a pilgrimage, magical places where illumination happens automatically at the right moment. God will find you wherever you are, when he sees fit, and in the way he considers most appropriate. Remember that, after all, Ignatius himself was an accidental tourist who had taken a detour to Manresa; nevertheless, it was there that the most important advances in his spiritual life took place.

The fact that so many Jesuit retreat houses are called "Manresa" hides an additional irony. We tend to think of retreat houses as places of consolation and peace. During his first phase in Manresa, however, Ignatius felt anxious and was disoriented. We can wonder at all the blessings with which he was finally graced, but we must also admire the intensity of his suffering.

He recklessly chastised his body: "He went through an

entire week without putting anything in his mouth" (*PJ*, p. 72). It is possible that such an extreme fast ruined his digestive system, since for the rest of his life he suffered stomach problems. He fought ferociously to eliminate every trace of vanity. He gave up the scrupulous attention he had paid before to his grooming and hair care: "he decided to let [his hair] grow naturally without combing, cutting, or covering it with anything either during the day or night. For the same reason he let the nails of his feet and hands grow, since he had also been overly neat with regard to them" (*PJ*, p. 64).

He was unable to free himself from the corrosive pangs of guilt regarding his past. Catholics are invited to unload the burden of sin in the sacrament of confession and to come out of it renewed and liberated: Go in peace and get on with your life! However, even after that written confession to which he had dedicated three days, guilt kept eating away at Ignatius. Though he understood the concept of absolution, he could not accept forgiveness. With great effort, he wrote out a new confession, an equally futile undertaking. He ended up contemplating suicide: "He was many times vehemently tempted to throw himself into a deep hole in his room there, which was near the place where he used to pray" (*PJ*, p. 70). But he always remembered that "it was a sin to kill oneself" (ibid.).

Just then, something extraordinary began to happen in Manresa. While still trapped in his self-destructive routine, "The Lord chose to awaken him as from a dream" (*PJ*, p. 72). Ignatius began little by little to develop the ability to read emotions, feelings, and the interior life, a spiritual "technique" that he would later call "discernment of spirits".

One element of this spiritual technique is to seek out the advice of impartial and wise mentors and guides. In Manresa

Ignatius found confessors who perceived his lack of balance and forbade him to subject himself to fasts or obsessive fretting over sins already confessed and pardoned.

Another aspect of his process of discernment was the careful heeding of his own inner voice, what we could call the "prayer instinct". Ignatius recalled, for instance, his experience in the tower house of Loyola, where his thoughts about knightly adventures excited him momentarily, though later they left him "dry and unhappy". Conversely, when he daydreamed about serving God, "he not only found consolation in these thoughts, but even after they had left him he remained happy and joyful" (*PJ*, p. 48).

Reflecting on these opposing sentiments and on the lasting peace that came over him with the thought of serving God, Ignatius ended up inferring a key element of his focus of discernment. When you ponder an important decision, he tells us, in prayer imagine yourself experiencing the different possible choices. Pay close attention to the thoughts and feelings that arise in you during and after the meditation. For example, if imagining one of the two professional paths you are considering appears always to leave you "dry and discontent", which was how Ignatius felt after daydreaming about knightly adventures, it is possible that you are experiencing "desolation", that is, a kind of "spiritual warning sign" that the option you are contemplating might not be the best next step for you to take in your life (or, even worse, that it might even be sinful).

As Ignatius formulated it in his *Spiritual Exercises*, desolation can bring "darkness of the soul, turmoil of the mind, inclination to low and earthly things, restlessness resulting from many disturbances and temptations".[2] On occasion,

---

[2] All quotations from *the Spiritual Exercises* are taken from *The Spiritual*

desolation leaves the person with a "loss of hope, and loss of love . . . completely apathetic, tepid, sad, and separated as it were, from its Creator and Lord" (*SpEx*, p. 130). Ignatius admonishes us not to make any important decision while subject to desolation; it is better, rather, to search out the roots of the uneasiness by digging more deeply into the thought process.

On the other hand, Ignatius felt "content and happy" during the times when he daydreamed about serving God and even after such daydreams were over: just the opposite of feeling desolation. To this inner indicator Ignatius later gave the name "consolation", which could be characterized as giving "courage and strength, consolation, tears, inspiration, and peace" (*SpEx*, p. 129). Consolation includes "any increase of faith, hope, and charity and any interior joy that calls and attracts to heavenly things" (*SpEx*, pp. 129–30).

Ignatius derived another valuable principle of discernment by analyzing with great attention to detail his own self-destructive impulse to submit to punishing fasts or to repeated recollection of the past. Earlier this had seemed to him something holy: Was he not demonstrating by it an intense contrition for his sins? But in hindsight, Ignatius realized that such compulsions harmed him physically and mentally and that God would surely never encourage us to harm others or to harm ourselves.

Thus, Ignatius learned (and later taught and continues to teach others through the *Spiritual Exercises*) that it is fundamental, though very complicated, "to listen to one's own heart." On the one hand, our inner voice, through feelings

---

Exercises of Saint Ignatius, trans. Anthony Mottola, with an introduction by Robert W. Gleason, S.J. (New York, London et al.: Image Books, Doubleday, 1964); abbreviated hereafter as *SpEx*.

of consolation or desolation, is capable of guiding us to the correct decision when we face a difficult choice. But we must also use our head, never only the heart. What is felt initially as consolation can turn out to be a temptation under the appearance of good, like the attraction Ignatius felt for self-destructive fasts. We all have blind spots; we find ourselves trapped in self-destructive patterns; we become addicted to certain vices and can be very clever when it comes to rationalizing our unhealthy choices.

That is why people who are good decision makers, Ignatius discovered, prepare themselves to pay careful attention to *both* the head *and* the heart, thereby creating a system of internal balance of powers. The ideas of Ignatius dealing with discernment are among the great legacies that he left to us modern people. Who does not have trouble making important decisions? And who does not feel torn between opposing inner feelings? The techniques of Ignatius help us to interpret our inner voice and to become, with practice, people who make their decisions more wisely.

The clearest sign that Ignatius was developing valuable spiritual ideas was the simple fact that, at a given moment, the inhabitants of Manresa began to ask him for advice, notwithstanding that here was a personage of pitiful appearance, who went around limping from one place to another dressed in sackcloth, uncombed and unkempt. Some of the townspeople nicknamed him the "sack man" or also "crazy for Christ". Be that as it may, Ignatius emanated an undeniable charisma; as he himself recounts, "he sometimes spoke with spiritual persons who respected him and desired to converse with him, and though he had no knowledge of spiritual matters, nevertheless, his words manifested a great fervor and a firm will to advance in God's service" (*PJ*, p. 68).

At a later time in his life, Ignatius recalled this age of Manresa and found in it the working of Divine Providence. In many ways, he did not know what he was doing, and he could have harmed himself; and yet, "During this period God was dealing with him in the same way a schoolteacher deals with a child while instructing him. This was either because he was thick and dull of brain or because of the firm will that God Himself had implanted in him to serve Him—but he clearly recognized and has always recognized that it was in this way that God dealt with him" (*PJ*, p. 74).

This may be the most profitable lesson of Manresa for all of us: to trust in God even when we cannot see clearly where he is leading our life, just as Ignatius had the feeling that God was directing him somewhere, though he could not see his way completely. Trust in God, and persevere through all the challenges, because God can find a way to work with us just as we are, dealing with us as a good schoolmaster deals with a student, as long as we are patient and open to learning.

The end of the beginning of the story . . .

The Ignatian Way ends formally in Manresa, and, consequently, this biography also ends there.

But, even though Ignatius considered Manresa the high point of his spiritual life, universal history focuses predominantly on the subsequent achievements of Ignatius; so in what follows we are going to reconstruct briefly the path that led him to found the Society of Jesus.

From Manresa, he arrived at Barcelona in February 1523, with the aim of continuing his travel from there to Italy, where he hoped to find passage on another ship to the Holy Land. The captain of a ship agreed to take him to Italy free of

charge on the condition that Ignatius procure his own food
for himself. So, Ignatius spent three weeks in Barcelona praying and asking for provisions. Just before embarking, he left
the few coins that he still had on a bench on the dock, because "he wanted to place his trust, love, and hope in God
alone" (*PJ*, p. 83).

The boat docked in Gaeta, on the west coast of Italy, and
Ignatius traveled over land some 110 miles to Rome, where
the pope blessed his plans to go on pilgrimage to the Holy
Land. Then he went to Venice, embarked on a ship that
took him to Cyprus, and there on another that left him in
Jafa (modern-day Tel Aviv), before he headed to Jerusalem
riding a donkey.

Ignatius endured eighteen arduous months of travel before
reaching his sought-after destination; nevertheless, he only
allowed himself to stay there for three weeks. The Muslim-
controlled Jerusalem was not considered safe, especially for
lone travelers, and even less so for penniless eccentrics like
Ignatius, who would go off once in awhile to one holy site
or another without any supervision. The Franciscan friars
who supervised the pilgrims informed them that "many others had had the same desire [to remain in those holy places],
and some of them had been taken prisoner and some of
them had been killed; his religious order was later obliged
to ransom those in captivity" (*PJ*, p. 99).

And so, Ignatius was deported. He had left Loyola with
one sole plan for a new life: to live and to work in Jerusalem.
"Plan A" had failed, and there was no "Plan B". However,
as so often happens in life, from the ashes of disappointment
new aspirations arise. His spiritual identity had only grown
stronger due to his unforeseen stay in Manresa; likewise,
only after being expelled from Jerusalem did he outline the
course that would determine the rest of his life: "After [he]
came to realize that it was God's will that he not remain in

Jerusalem, he kept wondering what he ought to do, and finally he was inclined toward spending some time in studies in order to help souls; and so he decided to go to Barcelona" (*PJ*, p. 104).

Five centuries of history unfold based on that decision, though neither Ignatius nor anyone else could have predicted it then. He remained in Barcelona for two years, studying grammar together with little children, struggling to master basic knowledge that he had not acquired in his infancy and youth. He was thirty-four years old. Others must have taken him for a fool who had wasted his life; and in his thirty-four years, he had already lived almost two-thirds of what was the life expectancy in the sixteenth century. Through it all, Ignatius persevered, though he could not have foreseen clearly then what course his life was going to take in the future. This is another aspect in which the life of Ignatius is a parable for us: in the end, we control no more than our attitudes and our behavior; we never really know when and how and at what moment of our lives opportunities are going to present themselves to us.

Ignatius continued his studies in Alcalá, Salamanca, and, in time, Paris, where he graduated as Master of Arts in the spring of 1534, almost a decade after initiating his formal studies in Barcelona. While studying in Paris, he met Francis Xavier, Peter Faber, and nine other companions, who together decided to found what they called the "Company of Jesus", approved by the pope in 1540.

And what about Jesuit history between 1540 and the twenty-first century? Paraphrasing the ending of the Gospel of John, if we had to write all that the Jesuits have said and done in these five centuries, it would be necessary to write a mountain of additional pages, too much for a backpacker or a cyclist to carry with him from Loyola to Manresa.

Pilgrimage, a preparation for life

The experience of pilgrimage marked Ignatius for the rest of his life. Decades after his trip from Loyola to Manresa, he would refer to himself throughout his autobiography, as "the pilgrim". His very sense of identity was forged on that pilgrimage.

And the pilgrimage of Ignatius marked the life of the Jesuits forever. The Jesuit *Constitutions*, the "rule" of the Society of Jesus, require that Jesuits in formation live the same formative experiences that one would expect of any seminarian: spiritual retreats, charitable work, training as a catechist, and so on.

But Ignatius added an absolutely unique twist to the formation of Jesuits, instructing the novices to go "spend another month in making a pilgrimage without money, but begging from door to door at times, for the love of God our Lord, in order to grow accustomed to discomfort in food and lodging. Thus too the candidate, through abandoning all the reliance which he could have in money or other created things, may with genuine faith and intense love, place his reliance entirely in his Creator and Lord" (*Constitutions* 67).

Thus, every year, Jesuit novices around the world set off on pilgrimage, thereby honoring the tradition of their founder, Ignatius.

As is made clear in the *Constitutions*, he insisted on the undertaking of this practice with a view to fostering a more profound trust in God. In effect, any Christian would *say* that he trusts in God; but, by sending the novices to the streets to beg for food and lodging, Ignatius wanted them to *feel* this faith in their bowels. The founder of the Jesuits was extraordinarily prescient, for the human instinct to trust completely in oneself has done nothing but intensify from the sixteenth century to our day. We, the conscientious moderns, fill our pantries, save for retirement, buy insurance, and take innumerable other measures—all unknown in Ignatius' time—to guarantee as much as we could need for today . . . and for all of our tomorrows.

But did Jesus not advise just the opposite? "Therefore I tell you, do not be anxious about your life, what you shall eat or what you shall drink, nor about your body, what you shall put on. . . . Look at the birds of the air: they neither sow nor reap nor gather into barns, and yet your heavenly Father feeds them" (Mt 6:25).

Jesus does not advise a careless negligence or an irrational hope that meals or pension plans will materialize miraculously just by trusting enough in God. Of course we have to take care of ourselves and our loved ones responsibly. But Jesus warns us that the devouring obsession to have everything under control can distort our priorities and even our relationship with God. We worry about earthly problems and lose sight of the purpose and ultimate spiritual destiny that should animate us. We run the risk of turning into the gods of our own life; that is, we focus constantly on our earthly needs, and we ourselves are the gods who satisfy such needs.

On the contrary, Jesus recommends: "Seek first his kingdom and his righteousness, and all these things shall be yours as well" (Mt 6:33; see Mt 6:25–34). Keep your priorities ordered correctly. Put God first. Pilgrimage fosters such a mentality, because no pilgrim can take his house, his closet, or his fridge with him, nor can he incessantly buy new clothes and electronic gadgets to stuff into tiny backpacks. What is more, unexpected setbacks remind pilgrims what tenuous control they have over life: one arrives at the town where he had thought to spend the night and finds that the shelter is already full, or one notices approaching storm clouds while traversing a stretch of the route with no place where he can take refuge. These small trials can yank us out of the "I control my world" mentality, pushing us toward the "Seek first his kingdom" mentality.

Ignatius also knew how to appreciate the practical value of pilgrimage: he needed resilient Jesuits capable of enduring deprivation. In one letter he laid it out unambiguously: "It might be said that whoever does not know how to persist and walk a whole day without food, and sleeping badly . . . will not be able to persevere in the Society."

When Ignatius wrote the *Constitutions*, he surely had in mind companions like Francis Xavier, who had endured treacherous crossings in rickety boats, drinking nauseating water, and eating moldy bread and meat on the verge of spoiling. And all of that before arriving at their destinations, often as the first Europeans to live in their host communities; once there, they had to strive to overcome loneliness and to come to master languages, customs, and religious beliefs that were not familiar to them in any way. It is not surprising that Ignatius would think that a novice pilgrim unable to endure lack of sleep and bad food could not be fit material for the Jesuits.

At a later time in Ignatius' life, his confidant Luis Gonçalves da Câmara asked him why he had included pilgrimage in the formation of Jesuits. Ignatius answered simply: "Because I myself experienced how beneficial they are and discovered how much good they did me."

The pilgrims who travel the Ignatian Way will probably come to the same conclusion.

3

Ten Lessons Ignatius Teaches

What can we people of today learn from the experience of Ignatius that will help us to recognize our own pilgrim's journey, whether on the road that leads us through Spain or on the road through life? Ten enriching lessons come immediately to mind:

1. Look around you

At the beginning of the second week of the *Spiritual Exercises*, Ignatius imagines the Holy Trinity looking at "the whole extent and space of the earth, filled with human beings . . . so varied in dress and in behavior. Some are white and others black; some at peace and others at war; some weeping and others laughing; some well and others sick; some being born and others dying" (*SpEx*, p. 69). And he goes on pilgrimage with this same attitude: taking note of the world's beauty, of its joys and sorrows. Do not limit yourself to traveling your Way remaining oblivious to the wonders and the sufferings of the world.

A pilgrimage is not a "task" that has to be completed as efficiently as possible. We often hurry from point A to point B, rushing from one class to the other or from meeting to meeting. We do not stop to smell the roses, or even to consider them, or to look at the sky that spreads out above them or at the immigrant workers who cultivate them or at the lovers who exchange them as gifts or . . . well, you know what I mean to say. Making a pilgrimage blesses you with one of the rarest goods in the modern world: time. Enjoy it! Look around you, and take in what you can.

2. *Get going . . . do not stop*

"A journey of a thousand miles begins with the first step." This silly truism has become a cliché because it conveys a valuable truth: you will not achieve anything until you try; you will not finish an ambitious task unless you start it.

During his recovery, Ignatius "spent much time reflecting on his resolution [to go on pilgrimage] and wished to be fully recovered so that he could set out on his journey" (*PJ*, p. 51). What a positive attitude! He could not wait to get going. We, on the other hand, often become slackers. We allow our initial enthusiasm for some project to wane because doubts arise in us: we think that it is not the right time or that we could fail or that we are not totally prepared.

Well, one is never totally prepared for anything in life. Neither will the perfect moment ever come. Every new job, every change of profession, every pilgrimage . . . implies some risk. It is possible to fail, to be humiliated or offended, to run up against a dead end or to make a mistake. So what? Most of those who have achieved something have also known failure, and many successful people have stumbled countless times.

Because any endeavor that is worth the trouble inevitably comes with difficulties, the maxim is not only: "Get going", but: "Get going . . . and do not stop." Persevere.

3. Free your mind

People today depend permanently on external stimuli. Ever-more sophisticated electronic devices emit music and films. We talk on the phone, we exchange electronic mail, text messages and tweets.

We are more and more adept at channeling external stimuli; however, it is harder and harder for us to tune in to our own thoughts. A six-hour walk may seem somewhat overwhelming. And, a six-hour walk without cell phone or personal music player? Impossible! Is it really? "Disconnect" once in a while from the external stimuli. "Turning off" the external sound track will allow you to tune in to your own inner voice.

You will survive even though you let several hours go by without obsessively devouring the news, sports scores, and phone and Twitter messages. Clean the daily confusion from your mind in order to create space for your own thoughts to bubble up to consciousness.

4. Keep a diary

When an idea occurs to you, jot it down. Ignatius started a diary during his recovery and continued it throughout his entire pilgrimage. Recall that he wrote some things down "in the book that he guardedly carried with him and that afforded him much consolation" (*PJ*, p. 63). It will console you (as it did Ignatius) to reread the notes of your diary every few days and see how the vague and embryonic ideas which blossomed in your consciousness have gotten sharper with time, thanks to the fact that you have battled with them to get them down on paper.

5. Be generous

In the course of his pilgrimage, Ignatius donated money in Navarrete, gave his clothes to a beggar, and surrendered his weapons in Montserrat. Above all, he renounced his social status and his identity as a knight, as well as his egocentricity. He let go of all of it. He traded his path in life, with which he was familiar, for uncertainty regarding his future. The same fears that would overtake any of us in similar circumstances must have occasionally tormented him. Is this going to be right for me? Am I moving in the right direction in life?

A lovely prayer contained in the *Spiritual Exercises* exemplifies the generosity that characterized Ignatius: "Take, O Lord, and receive . . . all that I have and possess. Thou hast given all to me, to Thee O Lord, I return it. . . . Give me Thy love and Thy grace, for this is enough for me" (*SpEx*, p. 104). What great generosity of spirit!

Try to be magnanimous (which is a synonym of "generous", though the Latin root of this term better expresses the attitude: "great of soul, of spirit"). Be "great of soul", and let go of all selfishness, all attachment, all addiction; any possession that might be preventing you from becoming the best version of yourself. Ignatius surrendered his sword at Montserrat, symbolizing by this his willingness to renounce his past, to the end of grasping his future. Is there something you would like to let go of, by way of an equally symbolic offering in Montserrat?

6. Start where Ignatius left off

Save yourself the unhealthy anguish of Ignatius by learning from his missteps. He punished himself with too many penances, self-hate, and suicidal thoughts. His soul, as he put it, was "still blind" (*PJ*, p. 56). He had to undergo terrible torment before accepting himself as he was accepted by God, in spite of his sinfulness and the imperfections that might have been weighing him down. With time, he ended up finding out what everyone in his right mind knows—that none of us is as bad as the worst we have done. In fact, we are good, blessed, and loved, as Ignatius himself writes in the *Spiritual Exercises:* "Consider how God dwells . . . in me, giving me being, life, sensation, and intelligence, and making a temple of me, since He created me to the likeness and image of His Divine Majesty" (*SpEx*, p. 104).

Heed Ignatius' hard-won wisdom and accept your own goodness as God's creation. Do not compare yourself to others or judge yourself, taking as your standard an idealized criterion that is not at all realistic; instead, focus on your own talents and the contribution that only you can make to the world.

7. *Make the pilgrimage at your own pace*

Adopt your own pace for walking—and meditating on—the pilgrimage. Joyce Rupp, author of books about spirituality, recalls that, during the first days of a pilgrimage that she went on, she had to rush continually to keep the pace of her companions. When she was left behind, she felt inept and she worried a lot; furthermore, as a result of pushing her body too much, blisters appeared on her feet. But both her body and her spirit healed as she adopted her natural pace and rhythm. As a title for her memories, she chose the fundamental lesson that she had learned on pilgrimage: *Walk in a Relaxed Manner.*

Give yourself a time frame loose enough to be able to

"walk in a relaxed manner". And do not just *walk* in a relaxed manner; *pray and reflect* in a relaxed manner, also. In
one of the spiritual exercises, Ignatius advises us not to pray
hurriedly: "During the contemplation on the 'Our Father,'
if he finds in one or two words good matter for thought,
relish, and consolation, he should not be anxious to pass
on, even though he spend the entire hour on what he has
found" (*SpEx*, p. 107). Pause where you find fruit, as Ignatius says elsewhere.

8. Be courteous and keep open to learning

"In their conversation, they began to speak . . ." This
phrase, seemingly so run-of-the-mill, is in reality one of the
most extraordinary of the autobiography of Ignatius, because his "conversation" was with a Muslim. In spite of all
the incentives for mutual hostility, the two travelers entered
into a respectful conversation.

Pilgrims meet new people every day. Be courteous. You
are a guest. Feel grateful for the hospitality of your hosts.
Respect their culture (even if you are Spanish, customs in
towns are different from those in cities). Savor the privilege
of living outside your world.

Of course, during a prolonged and draining journey, every pilgrim can lose his temper at some point, as happened
to Ignatius when the Muslim did no more than express his
opinion. Exhausted and exasperated, you become furious
with the waiter who overcharges you for a meal or with the
receptionist who gives you the noisiest room in the hotel.
You will find yourself in such situations; and if you cannot
maintain your courtesy, at least be as wise as Ignatius' mule:
Get away from the conflict before you stab somebody!

9. *Pray . . . your way*

My best teacher of prayer taught religion in high school. In Father Duffy's class, we sometimes meticulously analyzed Gospel stories, imagining what it was that Jesus was trying to teach his disciples, who often lacked the necessary insight to understand him. At some point in the class, the emaciated and cadaverous Father Duffy would raise his bony hand and say: "OK, stop . . . Talk to yourselves. Talk to God." And we, those fourteen-year-old boys, spent the next two minutes reflecting on the Gospel story of that day or on whatever preoccupation might be distracting us, preventing us from focusing on it. And then we told God what was on our mind. I do not remember Father Duffy giving a dissertation on prayer. But he had no need to do so. "Talk to yourselves, talk to God": this quite accurately sums up the notion of prayer.

Everyone talks to God in his own way, and it is likely that he does it differently at different times. I started each morning of my pilgrimage praying the Rosary, praying the beads for half an hour every morning as my bones warmed up, the sun came up, and, bit by bit, I woke up. I did not keep track of the decades. I simply tried to create a rhythm of prayer.

I also carried written down on a sheet of paper the names of those who had asked me to pray for them. Every afternoon I took out the list, ever more crumpled and dirty from the sweat and grime accumulated day by day, read the names one by one, mentally visualizing each person, and asked God to bless them with peace and happiness.

How did Ignatius pray during his pilgrimage? He does not say, but the *Spiritual Exercises* suggest that he prayed in every possible way; with good reason, the *Exercises* recommend

fixed prayers, like the Our Father, and prayers of intercession asking God for specific graces. On occasion, Ignatius
invites us to imagine ourselves as observers of the events
of the life of Jesus; other times he advises us to pray in a
coldly rational manner.

He advocated the use of different forms of prayer; so then,
you do the same, and pray in the way that seems appropriate
for the moment. Remember, though, the advice of Father
Duffy: "Talk to yourself, talk to God."

10. Confidence

As a rural priest whom I once met on a pilgrimage put it,
"If you look for God, he'll find you." But where, when,
and how God finds you may be very different from what
you were expecting.

Any movie director, for example, would have staged
Ignatius' mystical illumination in Montserrat rather than
Manresa. Montserrat, an impressive monastery sheltered by
steep mountainous peaks, houses the famous statue of the
Moreneta, or Black Virgin, before which Ignatius surrendered
his sword in a moving vigil that lasted the entire night. The
perfect setting for mystical visions!

However, the big ideas came to Ignatius in Manresa, while
he was sitting next to a lazily flowing river, identical to thousands and thousands of rivers that lazily flow through similar
places in any part of the world. The absolutely common-
place character of the picture points to the extraordinary
character of God: God can bless us and, in fact, does bless
us in places beautiful or plain, in turbulently charged moments or on deceptively tranquil days.

What is the underlying message here? The world is God's,

not yours. You would like God to speak to you in a lovely spot when you desperately need illumination or consolation or when nothing distracts you and you are open to listening. But God operates on his own time. Keep your ears and your heart open . . . and trust. If you look for God, he will find you.

Put another way: God is always present; it suffices that we open our eyes to see him. The nineteenth-century Jesuit poet Gerard Manley Hopkins pointed out that "the world is charged with the grandeur of God", impressive in a rainbow, but no less majestic in the subtle beauty of a seashell. The British poetess Elizabeth Barrett Browning, a contemporary of Hopkins, urges us in an analogous way to discover the God always clearly present and yet too often ignored:

> Earth's crammed with heaven,
> And every common bush afire with God;
> but only he who sees, takes off his shoes,
> The rest sit round it and pluck blackberries.

One of Ignatius' Jesuit companions pointed out that "he knew that he was being gently led someplace, but he did not know where." It is possible that this concept does not comfort us, modern people who are obsessed with control and want to know exactly where we are headed and how we are going to get there. But the sooner you accept that you do not have control over all the facets of the journey of your life, the more you will feel at peace with yourself.

Think of Ignatius: he comes home from the battle of Pamplona wounded, broken, defeated, apparently without a future. Even when he starts his pilgrimage, he has no idea where his new path in life could lead him. However, at a later time in his life, when he looks back at the twists and turns of his months of pilgrimage, he notices that the providential hand of God was constantly pushing him in the right direction. As he himself put it, "during this period God was dealing with him in the same way a schoolteacher deals with a child while instructing him" (*PJ*, p. 74).

Trust in God.

II

THE IGNATIAN WAY:
A HEALING PATH
TO FREEDOM

The Ignatian Way:
A Path for Contemplation

by José Luis Iriberri, S.J.

Many are the paths contained within the Ignatian Way, from exuberant nature in its material and corporeal expression to the mysterious intangible presence in its sacred spaces and in the majesty of its natural pathways or in the secret of personal relationships.

What the Ignatian pilgrim will discover along the way are lovely landscapes that vary in their colors and aromas, according to the different seasons during which they wish to live out their experience. The luminous spring green of the beech and oak trees or the mature green of the fields of grain that turn to gold as the days pass and the pilgrim leaves behind the Cantabrian Sea to approach the Mediterranean. Open fields and walls of stone, castles that speak of a different past, and large homes that display the wealth that the land offered to its inhabitants.

Rugged mountains in the Basque beginnings, from deep and lush valleys to hardly perceptible slopes walking along the gentle Ebro River as it runs through the Aragon valley. Vineyards in the Rioja that change their hues as the fruit ripens; lagoons and rivers that, with their constant presence throughout more than 250 miles of the Ignatian Way, a Way of Water; but also a Way of Dirt and Dust, as well as of asphalt, that aggressive surface which cannot be avoided, being a necessity of modernization and efficiency in transportation. Paths of loose stone that help us to contemplate the diversity between us, like those stones on the path. Paths of clay where the footprint stays forever. Paths among trees, and paths with nary a shadow.

Important cities offer pilgrims the necessary contrast in order to evaluate what is gained through quiet walking and, thereby, to evaluate the distance that separates our daily life from that which is now forming within us. To go from the solitary silence of the rural roads—very little traveled, to be sure—to the well-known hustle and bustle of the big cities represents for the pilgrim a challenge that calls him to integrate what he has experienced with this "real" world that he knows so well. In the small towns, the forced anonymity of the cities is transformed into the curiosity and friendly reception of the folks who feel solidarity with the pilgrim's efforts and come generously to his aid. It is characteristic of all beginnings that the surprise is evident in people's faces when you talk to them about the Ignatian Way; but this same surprise is the pilgrim's when he discovers that there, where he has come, others before him have already come and have talked about their Way. Something so new, and they are already talking about it? Well, yes: word of mouth spreads like wildfire. Thus is constructed the Way of Relationships, which leave their mark on the intimate diary of experience.

Human relationships, which intertwine; and also, of course, a relationship with experiences of the *sacred*, in six sanctuaries of the presence of renowned pilgrims through the centuries: Loyola, Arantzazu, El Pilar, Saint Peter Claver,

Montserrat, and the Cave of Manresa. Marian sanctuaries and Ignatian sanctuaries, three and three, tied together on one and the same route. Large sanctuaries with great flows of pilgrims; and others humble, keeping a low profile that perhaps is not necessary to continue keeping. Contemplate the faith that for centuries has been manifested in these places. Live their traditions in order to draw out part of the Spirit that dwells there. The Way of Sanctuaries.

And, lastly, the Way of the Rising Sun. The Ignatian pilgrim moves toward the new sunrise every morning. The sun that illuminates his steps, that shows the direction to take each morning. The sun that, like a new Star of the East pointing to the mythic Bethlehem, guides the pilgrim to that meeting with Jesus, risen from the night of death.

1. The Search for Healing: Motives at the Beginning of the Pilgrimage

What is it that prompts us to undertake a pilgrimage experience? Is there a special call that puts us on the way to a certain place?

In a general way, we must say that is how it is: a pilgrimage comes from a personal call, an invitation to leave the comfort zone where we habitually live and where we enclose ourselves in a series of routine customs, feeling life as "already known", repetitive. Sometimes, according to age and life experience, the sentiment that there is a lot to make up for is precisely the call that gets us going. Other times, the call arises in a situation of change, and, on occasion, it is a good way to deal with certain crises that have arisen and remain unresolved. The call to pilgrimage is a call to get out of doors, to experience the weather, to realize the value of taking on the present from one's own past and, in this way, focusing in on a new future.

It is also true that studies on the motivations of pilgrims who make the Way of Saint James show that many of them set out without knowing the real motive; some of them even affirmed having felt a kind of call from the Way itself to set out to walk. Friendship and going with family are also strong motives. There are few who consider a pilgrimage exclusively from the point of view of a physical challenge or as pure excursion. It is true that it passes through idyllic settings, worthy of a good excursion; but then there are the places of little scenic value or that, in their monotony, ruin all the charm. In view of this, the conclusion is that to become a pilgrim there has to be an inner force that speaks to us more of our spirit than of our body. Sometimes, though the pilgrim does not at first have a conscious motivation, something happens along the way that leads him to discover that hidden call.

The point of departure for my own pilgrimage was the experience of thirst. "I thirst": these words of Jesus, which Mother Teresa of Calcutta exemplified in her life, this very expression was the one that filled me during the first meditation and during the Eucharist celebrated in the Chapel of the Conversion of Ignatius in Loyola. That was my personal need: thirst for life, thirst for God, thirst for encounter, thirst for inner knowledge, and thirst for direction. The routine of worldly life tends to parch the spirit inwardly. Although feelings are alive, they lack the authentic spirit of life, the orientation that impels toward the true horizon of promised happiness. Yes, many times we feel that the past holds us in our present and that this puts in doubt the future that we imagine: Do I really want that? Why did I choose that? . . . I need guidance. And the present, adrift in doubts, does not quite satisfy us, does it? There is situated the thirst for God, the thirst for encounter with Jesus Christ, the model and guide of humanization. More still, thirst for the Spirit who is to guide us to the Truth.

And the fact is that we are all wounded beings by nature. We all bear that triple wound spoken of by the poet Miguel Hernández: with three wounds we come to the Way; that of Life, that of Love, and that of Death. Modern psychology corroborates what we are saying. It is a wound that manifests itself in many different forms but that has a common point of encounter in the sensation of empty dissatisfaction, of diffuse discontentment about a present that appears to us as received and not chosen, although we are conscious of having made many decisions about it. Wounded by routine and by the abandonments we have experienced. Wounded by incomprehension and failures. Wounded by those imagined fears that have twisted our lives. Wounded by drawn out and ultimately fruitless searches. Wounded by encounters that should never have taken place. Wounded by blows received, either through our blindness or that of others. Wounded by the many logical reasons that closed the doors to our growth and development as human beings in Love. Wounded . . . We are wounded beings, and as a psychologist friend told me when I questioned the existence of a wound in my life: If you do not want to recognize it, then do not; but that is not going to make your wound any smaller. Denying it is not going to help to heal it.

Pilgrimage can be described as an instrument of human healing: through its unique characteristics, a pilgrimage is an extended time of exertion of the person in his holistic conception. Body, mind, and heart, what we could call our material corporality (muscles, nerves, fluids, internal organs . . .), our intelligence (our cerebral hemispheres and the interneuronal spaces, their interrelations, the world of ideas, knowledge, and its points of reference . . .), and our emotions (awakened by perceptions and forms, interacting with our sensations, and expressed in a great array of feelings): all of this will interact within the pilgrim along his exacting way. Our wounds, as needs rooted deeply in ourselves and experienced in the heart, the mind, and the body, always with more or less intensity, surface in the succession of steps that create the personal way of each pilgrim. Within this inner *laboratory* is where the memories of the past are mixed with the sensations of the present and result in unexpected, surprising reactions, in which God himself has a hand.

Pilgrimage is *healing* because, without artificially provoking the encounter with oneself, with that which is sacred in your life and in others, this authentic encounter happens through the intrinsic nature of the proposed venture. But that which produces the healing effect in a radical manner is the experience of reconciliation, something very characteristic in the account Ignatius of Loyola gives of his own life. In effect, Ignatius, burdened with a past quite far from a model life, needs to find reconciliation for himself and sincerely seeks to do so in Montserrat, with his long, three-day confession, and later in Manresa, with his extreme mortifications that often bring him into illness. Ignatius himself recognizes that in his youth, even knowing the good that he was called to do, his actual life was a bad example for those who knew of him and his exploits. Returning to his hometown, Azpeitia, with the need to atone for this dark past would weigh on his soul for years. The pilgrim's return to his origins is one more phase of his personal healing process.

Reconciliation is the healing of the wound, its scarring over. Of course, very often a wound that has scarred over continues to hurt, but this is in an entirely different way and, above all, without any risk of infection. The pilgrim will return to his place of origin, marked no longer by an open wound but by recovered health and ready to set out upon new adventures. To be reconciled with the past, with those moments lived in pain or desperation. To be reconciled with those loved ones who perhaps are no longer near. To be reconciled with oneself, for the wrong turns and paths wrongly walked that have cut short one's own personal happiness or that of others. And also, perhaps, to be reconciled with God, whom we sometimes accuse of not being there, of abandoning us with his apparent lack of support in our times of greatest need. To be reconciled with that calling in which we have failed or perhaps not adequately answered. The pilgrim obtains all of this experience of reconciliation through the extraordinary encounter with that which is the *presence of the sacred* in his life. The experience of reconciliation is a foundational moment for the pilgrim: a new reality opens up in his present, and he thus feels the freedom and the strength to head out toward a renewed horizon.

Reconciliation is one of the fruits of pilgrimage; but the benefits of the healing obtained are multiple and very diverse. Nowadays it is well known that we are surrounded by mystery. Years ago, it was more problematic to speak of intangible energies in interaction with us; but today we, joined by the experimental sciences as well, can affirm that we live immersed in an intangible reality: if the visible physical universe signifies approximately only 4 percent of the whole universe, we must admit that we exist in and form part of an immense mystery that, surprisingly, we are capable of accessing through our mind, our heart, and also our sensory corporality. Modern medicine tends to view man as a total, a whole, in which the states of malfunction or illness have multiple causes that interact among themselves. In this way, the emotional world interacts directly with the materiality of our fluids and organs, and the mind, through its thoughts and ability to concentrate, can heal the sickness within us. Pilgrimage, which integrates the human being, can heal both the inner and the outer person. Pilgrimage establishes a dialogue between the parts of our being that have fallen out of communication and by doing so have provoked a disintegration of our being. The mind, the heart, and the body are not always in agreement and, sometimes, are even in clear opposition. To walk at an appropriate personal pace, to maintain a balanced effort through time, to leave a mental space far from daily concerns, to create an emotional distance that allows one to balance and serenely assess one's experience and relationships . . . , all of this together with the contemplation of the landscape and the reception of the multiple signals that we receive along the Way . . . All these God uses to heal us in the course of our pilgrimage.

It is a fact I have confirmed many times that pilgrims with strong pains, be it from tendonitis or from simple blisters on the feet, resist abandoning their Way because their inner strength sustains them. At the end of the Way, the healing within them is global: their legs, feet, and back are strengthened at the same time that inwardly they are pacified and reconciled. Gillian, another of the pilgrim champions of these words, explains that for her a key moment of overcoming pain and profound acceptance was precisely while awaiting the arrival of her fellow pilgrims, stretched out in a field of ripened wheat. The golden hue of the field, the azure of the sky, the silence that enveloped it, and the feeling of the lameness of her injured leg carried her to the inner peace of one who knows that she is reconciled with that unaccepted past, with that yesterday which still hurts after so many years. The inner healing allowed her to keep walking with the group, though taking the appropriate precautions and not going more than three miles at a time. With her negative medical prognosis, she arrived at Barcelona still on crutches, but she soon left them to fly back home without them. This real metaphor of the flight aids us in comprehending that at the end of the pilgrimage there is a *lightening of weight* that gives us new wings to fly freely.

2. Freedom Is Found at the End of the Journey

As the reader can perfectly understand, reconciliation is the source of freedom in all those spheres where this reconciliation has occurred. Freedom, in effect, is experienced inwardly but has very notable outward repercussions: the pilgrim who has conscientiously traveled the way, who has lived it with the required intensity, who from the start decided to enter into it, as Ignatius says in the *Exercises*, with a large soul and much generous freedom, receives in exchange, increased to unthinkable proportions, this same gift of freedom . . . And this is felt in the legs! One feels freed of one's baggage, with a spring in the step, moving ahead effortlessly, in good spirits, with a smile on the lips and a cheerful gaze. The pilgrim sings on the way, talks and plays with the other pilgrims. He freely shares his memories, now in a grateful way and without bitterness.

Freedom to live. In our case, speaking of the Ignatian Way, freedom to follow Jesus Christ, to orient ourselves to the mission. Saint Ignatius seeks constantly to be accepted by Jesus, to be on his *team*, and to build the Kingdom together. Following his experience in 1522, the pilgrim Ignatius looks for other pilgrims to walk the same Way, and from this is born the Society of Jesus, also deeply marked by the experience of pilgrimage, not only in the initial formation of Jesuits, but also in their own style of life. The freedom born from the experience of the *Spiritual Exercises* is a liberty that is active and ordered toward the Kingdom in such a way that it is committed to the construction of a new world.

The freedom experienced is also a mature freedom in the fire of the discernment of spirits, as Ignatius would say. And in fact, along the Ignatian Way the pilgrim will not lack appropriate times to experience and discern his spirits, his inner movements, his states of mind. The daily experiences penetrate the person, and in his inner laboratory deliberate decisions are developed.

On one occasion, some French pilgrims recounted to me, only a few days after they had experienced the event and still with tears in their eyes, the difficult moment they underwent on the highway when, nearing Montserrat, a motorcycle with two passengers skidded out only a few yards from them and crashed into the guardrail. The pilgrims were unharmed, but one of the riders lay inert on the road; the other was crying desperately some yards farther away. The pilgrims rushed to their aid. With a blanket and a mat, they tried to make the wait for the ambulance more bearable. An unexpected and traumatic situation. An hour later, they were able to continue their approach to the famous monastery, upset by the experience. They paused to breathe and relax, removed now from the police and paramedics who had come to take care of the victims. Seeking rest, they came across a family of Peruvian immigrants celebrating an anniversary. Amiably, these latter invited them to eat with them, and the pilgrims, amateur musicians, played songs for the family. What a contrast with the earlier scene! Finally, at the end of the stage in Montserrat, after they had gone through so much, came the culminating moment of the experience: inside the basilica, as they listened to the boys' choir and the monks singing and praying, the emotion of all that had happened surfaced, and in their inner awareness a new comprehension of life and death blossomed, which for one of them meant the peaceful acceptance of his mother's death years before. Reconciliation. That day and those moments in Montserrat were still very present in them when they told me about it emotionally days later.

The *inner laboratory* is always open in the pilgrim. What have I experienced? What am I experiencing? Where is it leading me? Why did it happen, or why is it happening? And it is the intention of Ignatius of Loyola that the pilgrim, by questions and discoveries, turn his free will little by little toward the greater good, the greatest. We do not settle for less if we can aspire to more. What am I going to do with my rediscovered life? What am I going to build with my new freedom? Ignatius thinks that every pilgrim who has understanding will end up offering to participate in the construction of the Kingdom of Righteousness, Peace, and Love that Jesus proclaims constantly to the hearts of all men and women. The French pilgrims were confronted unexpectedly with the meaning of a life that is gained and lost so easily. Ignatius lay in his sickbed wondering about the same thing. Life is worthwhile if it is put in the service of Love, and Ignatius discovered in Jesus, poor and humble, the model of this path.

Freedom draws strength from the experience of reconciliation. A Latin American pilgrim told me of long years of distancing in his relationship with his wife. One of the motives of his pilgrimage was precisely to find a way to reunite sincerely with her again. Disoriented, he looked to

God for a sign of what he had to do. Almost at the end of his pilgrimage, he marveled to discover that God asked him to do nothing, but to live with inner peace, reconciled, and to await his Presence in what happened. Not to be closed to anything and to receive with generosity and enthusiasm whatever was to come. In some way, he understood that by exchanging his anxiety for the peace of the Spirit he could be closer to the solution to his problem than by once again taking an approach already tried and failed.

3. Conclusion: We Become Pilgrims Forever

The transformation experienced is a lasting one. Ignatius of Loyola himself considered his life to be an ongoing pilgrimage, and he called himself "the pilgrim". And, as shown by the studies done on pilgrims' return home, the experience endures through time. Many recognize that their approach to life has changed, that there is less hurry, and that one values what one has much more. Different priorities are also formulated, and the experience of the Way is used as a metaphor to apply to daily life. One pilgrim says: "Life has taken me back to my job and to the routines of family and friends, but I have conserved the lovely spiritual change and the peace that I experienced on the pilgrimage. Indeed, I am surprised to feel how that change, in fact, slowly increases and spreads to many aspects of my life (it is that marvelous God of Surprises who continues to act)."

Some pilgrims explain that they have greater capacity to experience the presence of God, as if they had fine tuned an instrument for detecting God more and better in all things. For this it helps to experience the Ignatian pilgrimage at the hand of Saint Ignatius, through the gift of his autobiography, and to visit the places where he lived or had some of his experiences. In the words of one pilgrim, making the Ignatian Way can put flesh on the spirit, or, said another way, Ignatian spirituality can be experienced physically, through the encounter with history in those places significant for that spirituality.

Finally, it must be mentioned that fear of the future also emerges at the end of the Way; fear of the ability or inability to continue living what has been learned when one is in different surroundings, the habitual and routine surroundings. The pilgrims are about ready to go back home and are even ardently wishing to, like the disciples of Emmaus after their meeting with the Master. But they are not deceived: they know that the people with whom they are to go on sharing their lives have not had the experience of pilgrimage and do not have the keys of understanding that they have acquired. The pilgrim has been transformed, but his surroundings are the same as before. One of our pilgrims tells us: "We feel great, but we still have to come to terms with our return to the world, which has not changed! Our age group especially, now in the last third of our lives, seems to be searching for a greater spiritual meaning at this point in our lives. Penance, forgiveness, healing, and transformation are topics that come up very often in our conversations with friends and companions of the same age. The Ignatian pilgrimage gets right to the heart of these issues, which is why it adapts well to the needs of the people of our age group, the so-called 'Baby Boomers' in Australia."

I will finish with a note from my own experience as a guide on the Ignatian Way. Making the pilgrimage with the group, walking with them, sleeping in the same places, receiving the sun and the rain with the same intensity, eating at the same places, and sharing the moments of reflection, the silences and the Eucharists, the guide is not a guide only because of his preaching or his somewhat wise words, but also because of his gestures and attention to the pilgrims. Guiding a group of pilgrims in their Ignatian experience of the *Spiritual Exercises* is done through the whole person, in the same way that it is the whole person who is involved in the pilgrimage. The guide participates in the experience from his own situation and contemplates and accompanies the evolution of each of the pilgrims. The guide is a witness to the Presence and maintains attention focused on the objectives proposed in the *Exercises*. To be a guide on the Ignatian Way is a vocation.

The pilgrimage has been successful if, finally, the pilgrim can experience inwardly the difference between being a religious tourist and being a pilgrim. The testimonies that follow have achieved an appreciation for the difference.

When God Forgives Us,
He Really Does

by Sarah Davies

It is difficult to say exactly what led me to undertake the Ignatian Way at this point in my life, unless I consider that it was really God who knew that I needed it. In the middle of my career, at a time of transition in my professional work, I had arranged to enjoy a free period of three months when, out of the blue, I got an email regarding a pilgrimage in a small group, right in the middle of my planned rest. Then and there, I felt a strong desire to be a part of that trip, even before knowing precisely what it was about; and when I began to read and to talk with others about the pilgrimage, everything seemed to confirm my desire. It was evident to me that I wanted a change. In a way, I was already making changes in many of the external aspects of my life, and this proposal seemed the perfect opportunity to look within at my spiritual life.

I saw my spiritual director before leaving, and together we identified some of the things I expected from that experience: to strengthen my own confidence and my trust in God; to be able truly to understand in my heart that I am loved; and to accept the circumstances of my life, especially those aspects that I wished were different or easier. I had the hope that the pilgrimage would bring some kind of spiritual conversion or significant transformation; nevertheless, at the same time I felt a certain fear of what such a conversion could mean for the comfortable life I was leading.

At the end of the Way, looking back, I can see that through God's grace I have received all that I was hoping for . . . and more. My transformation took place little by little; there was nothing to be afraid of. On the contrary, the only small trace of fear that I felt, as I traveled back home, was the thought of being again dragged into my old way of being upon discovering that everybody and everything else continued to be the same!

What happened on my trip? I shared this pilgrimage with five other pilgrims for nearly thirty days, twenty of them covering a stage a day on foot. Together we followed the *Spiritual Exercises* developed by Saint Ignatius. Each day we spent the first two hours of the walk in silence, reflecting on the theme of the Bible readings for that day. After that, sometimes we got embroiled in serious discussions while we walked the Way, and other times we went along and shared stories, a laugh, a song, feeling sorry for our stiff muscles, pains, and blisters, or just walking together as friends. At the end of each day, we also shared our reflections and the Eucharist together, building our small community.

Getting energy from the land of Saint Ignatius and the love of God

We started in Loyola, in the home of Saint Ignatius' family, where the energy was palpable. I had recently read the autobiography of Saint Ignatius and was impressed by his story.

Seeing the places where he had been, both in Loyola and at other points along his pilgrim's route, created within me an authentic connection with the real person and the spiritual way we were following.

One of the first things we were asked to meditate upon during the pilgrimage was how emptiness is the condition for receiving. This related not only to some of the experiences of my life but also to the real beginning of this pilgrimage, since we had set aside and left behind a mountain of things that normally occupy our time and energies in order to open ourselves to this trip. I found that the more time we spent on the Way, the more the demands of home life faded and our daily life was extraordinarily simplified. As pilgrims, we were invited each day to walk, to reflect, to pray, and to be in the company of the others . . . And that was all we had to do.

The first part of the Ignatian Way is located in the Basque Country, which is green and lovely. Here it was easy to begin the exercises that lead us to meditate on God's love in creation and in our life. I have always liked to walk, especially in the countryside, in search of tranquility and feeling comforted by the beauty of nature. I tend to be someone who lives in her head, fretting too much about things. Freed from the daily tasks and my job, invited simply to walk, I found myself with lots of time simply to be myself. Having time to look at the past made me aware that I had received, though not always acknowledged, God's love in great abundance manifested through the actions of friends and family. This awareness opened within me a deep sense of gratitude, reinforced by the magnificent setting where we walked.

Accompanied by love, our contemplations during the first week were on sin and the great gift of mercy. In my diary I jotted down Romans 5:8: "while we were yet sinners Christ died for us." It is incredible how many times you can see or hear something and, in reality, you do not really fully get it. I felt like I began to get it at that moment: a slow process of assimilation . . . So, he died for me, and I did not deserve it . . . ! Nothing I do would make me deserve it. I can trust fully in the love and mercy of God, and with this confidence I can walk in liberty. When God forgives me, he really does, just as he says: he does not stay entangled in things, unlike what happens to me. I begin to see in myself that to remain in guilt, blame, grudges . . . can create the prison walls that rise up like barriers to being able to love.

Concrete episodes from one period of my life came back to me. Moments in which I felt a great desire to give myself in the service of others, though, strangely, I found myself without purpose and with a lack of empathy, as if unable to love the very people whom I had wanted to help. At this point of the pilgrimage, I know in my mind that God loves me just as I am, without my having to do anything to earn that love; but I recognize that I do not feel it fully in my heart. It becomes evident to me that, if I cannot completely accept that unconditional love, I can never hope to offer it to others. I saw it clearly: if I try to rely on my own resources without putting Jesus in the center and acknowledging his footsteps walking with me, I am going to end up burning out every time I try it. But something blocked me, and I would need quite a bit more time on this pilgrimage, peeling off layers, to arrive at the center of conversion in the heart.

Following Jesus with his love and going through suffering

In the second week of the *Exercises*, we are asked to contemplate the call of the King and the question of whom we are following. Our change of focus is reflected in the change of landscape as we advance from the green Basque Country toward the dryer and flatter wine region of La Rioja. I am getting used to walking and to living the pilgrim routine, in constant movement. We are asked to keep in mind that the call of Jesus is such that we cannot predict the stages through which our life journey is going to take us, and this seems underlined by our constant movement, advancing each day through unknown territory, following the Ignatian Way.

We reflect on the ministry of Jesus as that which acts on reality. I put myself in some of the Gospel scenes of his healing work, and I realize that I probably would have been reluctant to ask for Jesus' help, fearful of what he might ask me in return. But at the same time, I feel overcome with the sensation that it is completely useless to take any way other than that of following Jesus and being with him. The ways of the world do not bring true happiness, and they do not last. We have not brought anything into the world, and we cannot take anything with us beyond history. I have underlined in my diary the words of Jesus to Jairus: "Do not fear, only believe." And then also a two-line fragment of a favorite song of mine: "with love . . . but just do not do it alone", in this way newly connecting with my meditations of the first week.

The ministry of Jesus was countercultural in its day, as is the call of Christians today. Throughout this week I feel able to examine the large number of motivations and inner movements that arise on the way, discerning between what originates in the expectations of society and family and what does not come from there. I wish that all my intentions and operations could come from God and not from me. There are so many competing influences in life!

In the same way that our outer landscape changes on the way, upon entering the desolate and semi-desert mesa of Los

Monegros, the *Exercises* also move to a more somber territory, contemplating the price and the bravery, the suffering and the sacrifice of the way of Jesus. Reflecting on the pilgrimage of Jesus from Galilee to Jerusalem, on his journey toward the Cross, at the same time as we make our own physical and spiritual journey toward Manresa, some strong and significant connections occur. I saw parts of the story of Jesus on which I had reflected many other times in my life in a different way. I felt, much more intensely than ever before, the bravery and the value of sacrifice, and I think that for the first time I really understood that my choice to follow the way of Jesus could lead me to paths difficult to travel. I came to understand that I had unconsciously had an attitude of faith of the "superficial-optimist-dreamer" kind, believing that my faith would provide me with protection against the bad things we can experience in life, when the evidence shows that life does not work like that.

Contemplating the suffering of Jesus brought me to an important turning point in my own inner pilgrimage. I had the opportunity to enter again into the moments of my own life when I had felt completely alone and without strength, discouraged, and broken. Finally, I had the opportunity to recognize the root of one of those obstacles in my heart which prevented me from being able to accept God's love fully. I recognized that I still harbored a profound resentment and that I blamed God for a time when I felt he had abandoned me. I thought I had already arrived at an acceptance that reconciled me with that period of my life and that it was already accepted as an experience of personal growth; but the deeper examination drawn from this pilgrimage made me realize that those feelings still imprisoned me, preventing me from getting on with my life. I took this to the nightly Eucharist, and in the community prayer, at last, I felt at peace with that past time.

Of course, throughout that week I was growing deeper in the understanding of my call to follow Jesus. I had always felt a call to service, but often I have been so busy doing and serving that God has ended up in some way "out of the picture". Now I am more aware of being an instrument of God, understanding that I am not capable of loving people as I ought without the love of God, which flows through me without obstructions. Now, bit by bit, I am comprehending more fully that to dedicate my life to the way of Jesus does not guarantee an easy life but that I am never going to be alone on the voyage, regardless of how I may feel at times.

In the last week of our trip, we dedicated quite a lot of time to keeping in mind the life of God in all its plenitude, our journey toward freedom, new life, and eternal happiness. Reading the account of the disciples of Emmaus, I saw myself reflected in those men on the road, so enclosed in their ideas of how things should be and unable to see Jesus right at their side. I think about how we limit ourselves by trying to control our own destiny.

I reflected throughout that week on what it meant that my perspective on life had taken this turn, inward to outward, on this pilgrimage. In the past, I had often thought of my personal vocation as the duty to develop the gifts God had given me, realizing all of my potential. Now I think of my vocation as looking for the way to work together to build the Kingdom of God. I feel that it is an important change for me to move from focusing inward to looking outside myself.

Fog at the end of the Way

On the eve of our climb up to the monastery of Montserrat, I started to feel a bit sad thinking that the pilgrimage was coming to an end; but on the actual day of the ascent to Montserrat I experienced a very strong desire to return to normal life, but taking with me the new perspectives: to communicate the love of God; to build the Kingdom; not to be afraid; to be the person God loves, no matter what the world expects from me.

Once again, we had time in Montserrat to connect directly with the history of Ignatius, who, although in Loyola had entertained the idea of changing his life, saw his intentions confirmed during the prayer vigil realized in Montserrat and left here his sword and the clothing of his former life, making a gift of his clothes, putting on the pilgrim's apparel, and starting over. In the same way, we held our own vigil, praying the Stations of the Cross and sharing the Eucharist. That night, the station where Veronica wipes the face of Jesus was really a sign for me, a beautiful symbol of loving service that perhaps I may aspire to follow. I also left symbolically in Montserrat an object that belonged to me, as a sign of those things in my life that I want to leave behind, since I, too, am starting over.

We had not had much rain on our trip, but the day we went down from Montserrat to Manresa, our last leg, was gray and damp, and much of the mountain and the valley was darkened by fog. It seemed like an appropriate metaphor for my inner way: I felt I was taking a step toward the invisible and inscrutable future. During this leg I found myself again examining the question: "Do I know in my heart the God loves me just as I am?" And on this occasion, for the first time in many years, the answer is, "Yes."

In Manresa we visited the sites important to Ignatius, including the place on the hill that overlooks the city where it is believed he received his great illumination. In his autobiography, Ignatius says that he understood and perceived many things at this point: such great lucidity in comprehending everything that, if he took all the aid he had received from God and all that he knew and put it all together, it would not be as much as what he received on that one occasion.

Since I spent some time in that place, I was able to breathe it in deeply, feeling the sun warm my heart in my chest, contemplating a bird flying playfully in the wind, and feeling very, very happy; not in the sense of the happiness that is felt in the marvelous creation of God, which I felt in the first week of the pilgrimage, but a kind of full inner satisfaction. I know that outwardly my life can continue as before, but inwardly I am different; and this means that I am going to see all aspects of my life in another way from now on. I review these last weeks of pilgrimage, and I feel many small moments in which my eyes, my heart, my mind, and my spirit have opened to a new comprehension; my own little illuminations. I can feel my heart healed and that now I am willing to receive love. I feel completely free, free to opt for following the way of Jesus, no matter where it takes me.

Sarah Davies joined the International Red Cross a few months after her pilgrimage and was sent in service to the conflict of the Ukraine and, later, to Syria.

3

Seeing the Light after Thirty
Years of Serving Others

by Andrew Walsh and Gillian McIlwain

A few years ago, during a period of our lives when we were evaluating and questioning the meaning and purpose of ourselves, of our place in the world and of that of those around us, the two of us thought separately of doing a prayer retreat with the Jesuits. During the retreats, each one very different —one masculine, focused on those who are entering into the "last third" of their lives, and the other a silent eight-day mixed retreat—we liked and were attracted to the Ignatian approach to examining our lives.

At that moment, and at our age, we were looking for the renewal and reenergizing of the purpose and meaning of our lives. We had already done a large amount of self-reflection and psychological work; however, there was an element that was missing: the spiritual dimension that reflects the Christian values and practices with which we had grown up.

We had both arrived at a critical moment in our lives, right in that age bracket from fifty-eight to sixty-three years, known as the epoch in which people either regenerate or degenerate, whether by creating or taking new paths of freedom or by remaining trapped in the temptations of modern life and human expectations. We were at a moment when we wanted to gain perspective by looking back and taking stock of our lives, openly and honestly and with a depth that would reveal our true selves. Cynicism, pessimism, and doubt had wormed their way into us after we had worked many years in professional fields in which life is to be given to others who have been damaged, who have had problems, and who have often felt destroyed. At our sixty years, after having given more than thirty years to the service of others, we wondered why we felt so unsatisfied, disappointed, and unable to experience inner freedom.

It was not that we were unaware of our own personal needs in carrying out our work or of the wounds we were trying to heal within ourselves . . . It was, rather, the sensation of failure and that our inner spiritual being was imprisoned, trying to find a way toward freedom.

We had followed the advice, the rules, and the regulations; we had good families; we had good friends, but in some way we had gotten off track; we had achieved great successes, and we had also known personal sadness and regret, including the great question: Why? And how is it that I ended up like this, because it was not where I wanted to be and it was not who I knew I was?

Getting ready to challenge the past and to prepare the future

With this inner restlessness and these misgivings, we searched for a way in which we could challenge forcefully and authentically the old image of ourselves. Initially, we had the idea of doing the French Way of Saint James, knowing that a long trip, with a physical challenge and removed from our habitual life-style, far from distractions and seductions, would be the only way to find the space and the time to breathe deeply and untangle our inner selves. However, the French Way did not attract us sufficiently: it lacked something we could not put our finger on. We talked to a lot of people about their pilgrim experiences, but their description of the inner and outer voyage seemed to lack a critical element. Finally, and individually, during a retreat with the Jesuits we came across the Ignatian Way.

In retrospect, the time we devoted to the preparation for our pilgrimage, attending information sessions, preparation through courses of adult education dedicated to learning meditation on the way, and so on, was much more important than it seemed to us at the time . . . In fact, we had begun our pilgrimage long before arriving in Spain. In our Australia of origin, we focused, organized, and prepared . . . But, to our surprise, suddenly what we had planned was canceled due to circumstances beyond our control . . . and it was just then, when it disappeared from our horizon, that we realized how much this pilgrimage had already begun to mean to us. We did not lose heart and looked for a way to get to Spain on our own and to make the pilgrimage possible. The whole world told us that such a thing was not going to happen, but again the hand of God directed us to the right people, who made the pilgrimage possible. Everything fell into place, and we knew that it was going to be possible, even though we were a small group. This obstacle course already got us into our spiritual pilgrimage before we even left Australia. And little did we yet know how important it would be to keep breathing well on the difficult stage climbing up to Arantzazu! It seemed clear to us that we were being prepared by a mysterious hand to undertake a trip that would be a challenge at once fearsome, joyous, and liberating.

Without time to prepare, reflect, and plan out the pilgrimage, our arrival at Loyola would have been very different. Although at that time we thought we knew what we were looking for, the Ignatian Way was about to show us that there was much more to discover. Walking was not simple; it was not like a tranquil stroll through the fields on a sunny day. It was an arduous task; demanding, boring, exhausting, and discouraging. It brought many blisters, sore feet, and a marked feeling of vexation on many occasions; but it also provided us with great happiness, enormous satisfaction, and, finally, when the walking was joined with our inner voyage, the rhythm of the pilgrimage brought much peace, as we felt at each step the connection with the land and the opportunity to meld ourselves with nature, the sky, the trees, the birds . . . and to see things from a new perspective. Every day we walked through this world of God, contemplating its majesty and that grandeur which takes your breath away.

Walking with Ignatius toward inner space

To walk in silence every day gave us the opportunity to listen to the rhythm of our own footsteps as well as the opportunity to attend to our fellow pilgrims and also time to contemplate and reflect on those who had trod the way before us, especially the model of Saint Ignatius as he struggled with his own past, his shame, his guilt, and his fears. Our inner voyage was reflected in the outer voyage: draining, wounding, grueling, and many times frustrating. Taken together, the physical way offered us the enormous open space and the freedom to let the entire inner world rise to the surface, and thus the opportunity to examine it within the framework of the *Spiritual Exercises* of Saint Ignatius. In the same way that he advanced and grew in his love of God, likewise, as we meditated, the light on our own past grew within us, and we discovered how God looked at us and how we had seen him in our lives. Daily, our time of nocturnal reflection offered us a safe space to externalize these inner joys and torments of the Way, while the daily Mass gave us the opportunity to open ourselves before God and to enter into communion of spirit with the others, to cure gently the obstacles of the day as well as the disturbances of our souls.

Walking cures wounds: the body feels better with itself, and the soul becomes freer to elevate toward space and, from on high, to look every day, with God's eyes, at the world around us.

4

A Path toward Inner Happiness and the Freedom to Continue

by R. B. Riyo Mursanto, S.J.

I had been told that someone so ambitious as to become a provincial must be crazy. At the end of my six-year period as Jesuit provincial, I understood the meaning of these words well. I experienced a great sensation of relief. It is madness to desire a position that brings a heavy burden, both physical and psychological. I was aware that some people had become angered due to my decisions. Some had accepted them, but some suffered bitterly because of the decisions I thought had to be made. Upon finishing my term, I felt a kind of inner sadness, and I was sorry to have caused many difficulties in the lives of so many people. Certainly, to be a Jesuit provincial was not an easy task.

I was at one time in the highest position in the province. I had everything that corresponds to the Number One. People showed me great respect, special receptions, the first row in reserved seating, the best view, the special place to lodge and to eat, and any other thing that is offered to a V.I.P. But something impressive and unique in our Jesuit organization is that, after being number one, you have to be willing to be like any other person and even become the lowest of the low, if that is necessary. You can go from being "someone special" to being a "nobody". I mean to say that we do not cling to the elevated position, but that at any moment we are to be ready to serve, willing to be sent anywhere, to the place where the needs are greatest. An ex-provincial is to request a new destination from his successor with complete docility. Mentally, I was very clear about this; however, in my heart, there was a kind of uncertainty: Would I be free to request a new mission with complete docility?

On September 21, 2014, after completing the transfer of responsibilities to the new provincial, I began the Ignatian Way, bringing from home all those feelings in my heart. Between leaving Loyola and arriving at Manresa, I walked alone with God, on foot, for more than 410 miles. Burdened with my self-accusation for the many faults committed, with the conviction of having wounded many hearts, with the uncertainty about the future, with many questions, walking and trying to figure out in advance the new destination that my Jesuit superior was going to assign me, about which I had no idea. I was only sure about one thing: I wanted to walk following the footsteps of Ignatius; alone or, if I was lucky, finding friends on the way. My plan was not perfect. I do not speak Spanish, and it was the first time I had embarked upon the Way, of which I had only a simple description and the GPS route, without a clear idea about where to lodge, either. I carried the printed information of the entire Ignatian Way, downloaded from the web. That was all.

With much hope and in great spirits, ready to face anything on the way, carrying my inner burden, I began the Ignatian Way. My pilgrimage can be understood as an application of the four weeks of the *Spiritual Exercises*. Based on my own experience, I have expressed those four weeks in these four phrases: (1) "I am afraid and I cannot"; (2) "I want to"; (3) "I am ready to do it"; (4) "I feel happy and ready."

The first phase: "I am afraid and I cannot"

The first day I made a mistake navigating the route: Was I supposed to go straight, turn to the left, or turn to the right? All told, it was not a fatal mistake, and at last I found the right way to get to Zumárraga. There were people on the road doing physical activities whom I could ask for directions. But when I entered into the forest, climbing up through the lovely mountainous scenery of the Basque Country, I no longer ran into anyone. I was completely alone; alone with God. I could not ask anyone; only consult the description and verify on the GPS. My heavy backpack caused a blister on my right shoulder and consequent pain and tension in my back muscles. The winding trail, the rain, the cold of the fog, the mud, the back pain, the heavy pack . . . I began to imagine many more difficulties that awaited me on the way. I felt forced to stop, to think things over, and I said to myself: "I am scared and I cannot go on." Experiencing this sensation, carried away by the difficulties, I connected my mind with my Jesuit companions at home; with what they might have felt; with their experiences, perhaps much more difficult, upon carrying out their tasks stemming from my decisions. My physical difficulties were in reality much smaller compared with the psychological fatigue that my Jesuit colleagues had to endure due to my governing style and because I did not provide them with my personal support. Would they forgive my past errors? I was very sorry and felt a deep sadness thinking that they would not. But then I became aware that what I was experiencing on this Way was just the opposite: I was feeling the presence of God, who accompanied me at all times, even though I was walking alone. God does not count my sins and my mistakes. He always offers a new route toward the future, renewed hope.

The second phase: "I want to"

On the fifth day, according to my pilgrimage plan, I was to lodge in a small town: Genevilla. The only available bed and breakfast for pilgrims is called "Usategieta", but it was closed. The people advised me to retrace my steps and go two and a half miles back to the previous town, Campezo, and spend the night in a hostel. But going back two and a half miles would add five more miles to my way, counting the following morning. Instead of going back, I decided to advance to the next town, Cabredo, two and a half miles away, though I knew the problem would be the same: there was no guarantee of finding lodging. It was already dark. The only place open and illuminated, with people inside, was a small bar. I asked about the possibility of spending that night in the bar, but, understandably, they refused. Very reasonable. A kindhearted man offered to take me in his car back to Campezo. I calculated again: the five miles back meant adding more miles to the way, already in fact quite long. It was too much time. I was lost in thought when the miracle happened, made possible by my earlier conversation with them, using words that resembled Spanish and a lot of body language, since my Spanish is nonexistent. They understood, in fact, that I was not a dangerous person, though I came from Indonesia, a country with a Muslim majority. I think that, since I was from Indonesia, they thought that I was Muslim. But I said: "I Jesuit, no Catholic." I wanted to convey to them that I was more than Catholic: Catholic first, but, in addition to that, Jesuit; that is, that I was not dangerous. Trying to convince them, I proved to them my identity as a pilgrim. Once they were satisfied with the explanations, they seemed happy to know that their town was on the route of the Ignatian Way, which they had never heard spoken of before. They took me to the Civic Center of Cabredo, where I could sleep on top of the tables in one of the meeting rooms. In the morning, two women in the bar offered me two cups of coffee with milk for breakfast, along with biscuits and pastries.

Following this experience, feeling so well accepted by people completely unknown to me, feeling their kindheartedness, I summoned the courage and the confidence to put aside my worry about finding lodging and my thoughts of phoning my fellow Jesuits for help. The fear I had felt, the worry, were transformed into the intense desire to go ahead. The phrase, "I am afraid, I cannot" had now become "I want to do it." This is how I entered the second week of the *Spiritual Exercises*, to respond to the call of the Eternal King and walk under the banner of Jesus, just as Ignatius wrote.

The third phase: "I am ready to do it"

Do you believe in angels? We very soon forget the lovely experiences of our youth when, very serious and in secret, we talked and played with our guardian angel. I continued my pilgrimage on the Ignatian Way, leaving behind the mountainous region and entering into the relatively flat area of La Rioja, Navarre, and Aragon. When I had passed the halfway point of the Way, I stopped in front of the church of Saint Michael, in Fuentes de Ebro. For the first time I met with another pilgrim who was walking in the same direction as I was, to the southeast. I had already passed quite a few pilgrims walking to the northwest, toward Santiago, but I was going against the flow. This man was going alone and was sitting on a bench, rolling a cigarette. I went up to him and greeted him. He introduced himself as Raphael, from Poland. Can you believe that I met a Raphael in front of a church named after Saint Michael? Both are names of archangels, the messengers of God. Instinctively, I felt that the Lord had sent me an angel. I felt that Raphael was sent to me as my companion on this stretch of the Way. What happened after a brief conversation? He continued on his way, and I spent that night in the hostel of Saint Michael. The next day, now in the well-known desert of "Los Monegros", one of the semi-desert regions of Spain, Raphael popped up by surprise from the ruins of what had been a shepherds' refuge. I celebrated this unexpected encounter, and while we walked, he shared with me his experiences of sleeping in the fields, in the outdoors, and the way to position the backpack to be more comfortable and so as not to hurt the back. He told me that he had begun to walk three months ago. Bored by the route of Santiago, with too many pilgrims for his taste, he decided this time to walk in the opposite direction, from Santiago to Montserrat. I learned from him how to find a good place to stay in the fields under the night sky. Thus appeared the phrase that describes the phase of the third week of my spiritual exercises: "I am ready to do it." That night I was willing to run the risk of sleeping in the desert, in unknown territory and under a new sky, in my solitude. Yes, I was willing to run risks in my life. Raphael went on his way and disappeared over the horizon. I decided to stop and spend that night alone in the desert, under a lovely clear sky. I never ran into Raphael again. Was he an angel? I had run into him twice, and then only for a few minutes. In following Jesus, we not only have to say "Yes" to his call, but also have to be willing to take on any risk stemming from his mission. This includes the will to walk on his Way of the Cross.

The fourth phase: "I feel happy and ready"

Both experiences—that of not finding a hostel, but ending up sleeping in a meeting room in a Civic Center, and that of my solitary night sleeping under the sky of the desert— offered me the key for comprehending a new meaning of the protection and the love of God. *Providentia Dei* (the Providence of God) was a very real experience during the Way. I also remember the hospitality of the four Jesuit communities (Logroño, Tudela, Zaragoza, and Lleida) on the route to Manresa: they accepted me as a true friend in the Lord. Even more meaningful were the aid and the greetings on the road from people who did not know me at all. God gave me another friend, a seventy-three-year-old German, Mr. Eberhardt, the only Ignatian pilgrim I found doing the same Loyola-Manresa route. He appeared on the eighteenth day of my pilgrimage, and I ran across him only on three occasions. Later, he stopped off in Lleida, and I continued on to Palau d'Anglesola.

Once I had conquered the experience of staying alone in the desert and with the happiness of seeing myself supported by my Jesuit brothers and other people on the Way, I entered into the phase of the fourth week of the *Spiritual Exercises*. The phrase was transformed into this other: "I feel happy and ready." I felt happy as a Jesuit, enjoying the unique opportunity to do a sabbatical year traveling the Ignatian Way for twenty-seven days. I was sure that I had the privilege of being the first Jesuit from Indonesia to experience the Ignatian pilgrimage alone and on foot. I felt willing to go ahead, finish the Way, and to receive a new mission from my provincial at the end of my sabbatical year, whatever it was.

The stage from Igualada to Montserrat was not easy. It is a long stretch, steep and winding. But, knowing that Montserrat is the place where Ignatius had abandoned himself completely to God, dressing himself simply with a pilgrim's cape, I felt the determination of Ignatius to walk with more energy. The rhythm of my footsteps was even faster than in the stretches over flat land or on the paved road. The inner happiness impelled my legs, sprightly climbing the rocky path to the most visited Benedictine monastery of Spain. It was also the moment for me to experience happiness, after leaving behind all of my inner burden, all sadness and worry. From the mountaintop of Montserrat, I walked at last toward the valley of Manresa with my heart full of light, full of happiness.

The whole Ignatian Way was a walk full of grace. Beginning in the Chapel of the Conversion, where Ignatius spent his days of recuperation after being wounded, and finishing in the Chapel of La Cova, where Ignatius spent many days and nights meditating and writing down his spiritual experiences. At the beginning of the Inner Way, Ignatius started with harsh penances, but he concluded his Way by surrendering totally to the will of God, ready to be sent on his mission without conditions. I also began my pilgrimage penitent and burdened with my worries and uncertainties. Can we remain free from uncertainties with respect to our future? No. Nothing is certain in our life, except the certainty of the end of life when death comes to us. But on the

Ignatian Way I learned that, always following Jesus, we have hope, which encourages us to face any risk. Happiness is not found at the end of our pilgrimage as a free prize; rather, it is the result of facing many difficulties on the way, knowing that God's love and assistance can always be counted on. The heavy burden of the backpack expressed my own fears. But, in the end, bravery and hope helped me to overcome the obstacles on the way. From Manresa, I continued my way, now not on foot, but by train to Barcelona and from there to many other places until returning to Indonesia. I took back home the gifts and graces received from God: health, happiness, and the inner freedom of movement, accepting the new destination as a Jesuit when I receive the notification. I am content to have experienced existentially the sensation of "I am afraid, I cannot", and the subsequent change to the phases "I want to", "I am ready to do it", and, finally, "I feel happy and ready." I accept all that God might ask of me: I am ready to do his will. AMDG (Ad Maiorem Dei Gloriam).

5

My Conversion on the Ignatian Way

by Michael Smith, S.J.

In September 2013, I accompanied a group of twenty pilgrims during the 426-mile pilgrimage route initiated by Saint Ignatius of Loyola in 1522 from his place of birth in Azpeitia, in the Basque Country, to Manresa, in Catalonia. We covered practically the same route as Ignatius, going through many of the same cities he passed through, praying in the churches where he prayed, and marveling at the same natural beauties that he contemplated.

I would like to say that it was a great success and to explain all the good that there was . . . but this time I am going to speak about my personal failure on the Way and how it became an experience of conversion for me.

Our days were quite structured. Each morning, before we began to walk, we met at about eight in the morning outside the hotel where we had stayed, and I commented on the points of the *Spiritual Exercises* to be prayed during the day. Then we walked the first two hours in silent prayer. At night, we celebrated Mass and shared our experiences from the day during dinner.

Walking through your thoughts,
accompanied by suffering

To go on pilgrimage on the Ignatian Way manages, in some way, to put your head in its place. Kierkegaard says something to the effect that, above all else, the desire to walk must not be lost. Through this exercise, one enters into a state of well-being. This philosopher said that his best thoughts arose on the road and that he knew of no thought so troubling that he could not in some way remove himself from it by walking. Just by staying on the move, everything will be all right.

Well, I tried to follow this advice; but, unfortunately, everything was not all right. The first eight days of the Way, which are very demanding physically, passed by with no problems. Then, on the ninth day, we had a day of rest in the city of Logroño. Following the day of rest, we embarked on a long and, as was later seen, disastrous stage of the Way from Logroño to Alcanadre. As we were walking through the streets of Logroño, I began to feel a sharp pain produced by a series of cramps in my right leg. I thought I would be able to conquer the pain and keep walking, but I could not. As the day went on, I started to feel the same pain in my left leg. Walking was unbearable. After seven and a half miles, we arrived at a small town. I wanted to take a bus, a taxi, or a train and, in this way, get to our lodging in Calahorra; but there was nothing available. There was no choice but to keep walking. After five and a half miles, we came to another town. There were still no taxis. So again I had to keep walking. I walked the entire eighteen and a half miles suffering the same pain. We left Logroño at 8:20 in the morning, and it was 6:10 in the evening when we reached our destination. We were on the road for almost ten hours. It was a very long and painful day, which was possible only with many applications of Voltaren gel on my legs, several pills of Ibuprofen and Panadol, as well as the emotional support of my pilgrimage companions.

I woke up the next morning feeling a lot of pain. It was even difficult to stand up after getting out of bed. I could only limp. I had proposed to walk the full length of the Ignatian Way, but I knew perfectly well that it could cause serious long-term injuries if I continued walking. So I took a rest day in the hotel, with ice packs on my right shin to reduce the swelling. When the other pilgrims resumed the way, I was overcome with a profound feeling of loneliness. I also felt failure. I could not walk the full distance whereas the others could. The group went ahead without me. I felt frustrated for not reaching the goal and ashamed of my weakness. I needed six days of rest, a visit to the hospital, and a little physical therapy before I was able to walk again.

"Jesus, I need you to be my companion today"

The morning I resumed the Way with the other pilgrims I felt deeply apprehensive. Would I be able to walk the whole stretch? Or would my body give out on me again? When we started our march, I found myself saying to Jesus: "I need you to be my companion on this stretch." The meditation that accompanied this day was precisely the contemplation of Jesus in his Passion. For this meditation, Ignatius proposes in his *Spiritual Exercises* that we ask God for this grace:

"In the Passion the proper thing to ask for is grief with Christ suffering, a broken heart with Christ heartbroken, tears, and deep suffering because of the great suffering that Christ endured for me" (*SpEx*, p. 93).

The two last words, "for me", are crucial. Ignatius uses them carefully and deliberately, because he wishes the pilgrim to be aware that the terrible events that are unfolding in the Passion are an act of love "for me".

While we walked in silence during the first two hours of the march, I was filled with a profound inner sensation that Jesus was with me and loved me. While I walked with Jesus that day, I experienced with great feeling that he was making his way to Calvary for me, that he was suffering for me. I felt consoled and supported. I had never before had the sincere knowledge that Jesus really died for me, something that I perceived clearly that morning. That was my experience of conversion.

When I look back, I realize that, if I had not had the cramps in my legs, if I had not failed in my goal to walk the whole Ignatian Way, if I had not felt ashamed of my failure, if I had not been full of apprehension, then I would not have needed Jesus as my companion, I would have been sufficient by myself and, probably, I would not have received the grace of the inner knowledge to feel sincerely that he died for me.

My Way was not about success or failure. It was about recognizing my total dependence on God. The pain and the failure opened me up to God. I recognized my limits, and I found myself in the presence of Jesus.

A Way of healing that means going back home

I would love to be back on the Way, to put on a pair of boots and walk the roads of Spain in search of God and of myself, but I cannot. I have responsibilities in Australia. A story helps me to quell my desire:

In the tenth century there lived a man who dedicated his life to pilgrimage. He walked thousands of miles until finally, in his old age, his legs said to him "Enough!", and he retired to a monastery hidden in the mountains to obtain a well-deserved rest.

Though he never looked for it, he gained the reputation of being one of the wisest men, if not the wisest, in the known world. As a result, many young pilgrims from all over began to come to him seeking advice.

One day, a young pilgrim arrived at that monastery. In spite of his youth, he had completed the majority of the known pilgrimages. He approached the old man and asked him: "Master, what must I do to be a true pilgrim?" The old man looked him in the eyes and felt compassion for him. "Son, if you really want to be an authentic pilgrim, go back home with your family, your neighbors, your friends, and your enemies. Listen to all of them, put yourself in their service, forgive them, and love them. In this way you will become a true pilgrim."

They say that the young man lowered his eyes; he turned and left without saying a word, deeply saddened because, whereas he had been perfectly able to walk thousands of miles, even with a heavy load on his shoulders, he felt unable to carry out what the wise old man had proposed to him.

Our principal task is to listen to, serve, and forgive our families, our neighbors, our friends, and our enemies. If we learn to serve, forgive, and love, we become true pilgrims.

I would like to finish with a prayer by Thomas Merton:

My Lord God, I have no idea where I am going. I do not
see the road ahead of me. I cannot know for certain where
it will end. Nor do I really know myself, and the fact that
I think I am following your will does not mean that I am
actually doing so. But I believe that the desire to please you
does, in fact, please you. And I hope I have that desire in all
that I am doing. I hope that I will never do anything apart
from that desire. And I know that if I do this you will lead
me by the right road, though I may know nothing about
it. Therefore I will trust you always though I may seem to
be lost and in the shadow of death. I will not fear, for you
are ever with me, and you will never leave me to face my
perils alone.[1]

In the name of the Father, and of the Son, and of the Holy
Spirit. Amen.

[1] From Thomas Merton, *Thoughts in Solitude* (New York: Farrar, Straus &
Giroux, 1999), 79.

6

A Way of Healing—
My Ignatian Way

by John N. G.

My main motivation for becoming a pilgrim on the Ignatian Way is born of a conscious decision to try to rediscover my life and to deal with its dysfunction. The celebration of the Eucharist in the Chapel of the Conversion in Loyola, before setting out, strengthened my initial resolve: to live and to love freely and fully. To say this is easy, but to keep it present in real life can only be a grace from the Divine. For me, it is a matter of an ongoing navigation through the seas of the spirit in my self-process of growth, living real life, experiencing the tension of mixed feelings and the dismay that follows, the overcoming of deeply rooted bonds and the responses to the patterns of life, the struggle with the wounds of the past, its fears and insecurities. Following the footsteps of Saint Ignatius, I prayed from the heart and invited Jesus to walk with me, with my inner child and his wounds. I live today with the hope of having reached a real cure and that necessary conversion without which I do not see that there is a way to live and love, freely and fully.

Compiling insightful lines from his personal diary.

The thorns of life and the farewell to Arantzazu

We finished our demanding stage welcomed by the Sanctuary of Arantzazu, where Saint Ignatius also arrived in 1522 after his conversion and on his pilgrimage to Montserrat. We marveled at the faith of the souls who had collaborated in the construction of this amazing architecture. I almost anthropomorphized the modern basilica as if it were a good friend lost and found, my same age, with three pointed towers representing the spikes of the thornbush. Arantzazu signified for me "a place full of thornbushes—the symbol of life". I was touched by my reflection: the pain induced by the thorn was converted into the source of life. It did not happen to me at that moment, but the image of the inner change of Ignatius in that night of vigil in the sixteenth century continues to be vividly near and consoling for me.

Saint Ignatius bid farewell to his relatives in Arantzazu. The words that our guide said to us—"We are also going to say good-bye to Arantzazu"—kept swirling within me during our uphill trek, through a vigorously green forest that let the morning sun filter through. I continued saying good-bye to those parts of me that I did not like and that remained in me linked to moments of shame, wounds, and pain that either I had inflicted on others or other people had caused me. The process was reiterative and one of continual inner cleansing. I prayed at Erroiti, the legendary spring where the shepherd Rodrigo de Baltzategi found Our Lady of Arantzazu. Yes, I asked the Virgin to heal my hurts and wounds. I prayed to the freshness of the morning forest to purify them into sacred wounds.

Breathing deeply and accepting the mud

The descent toward Araia overlapped with the Camino de Santiago and some Roman paving stones eroded by cartwheels. As I went cautiously down through the forest, the path became rougher and muddy. Suddenly, I found my heart beating very rapidly. I almost lost my nerve as I concentrated so hard on my steps. This was a timely reminder of the traps of life that were strangling me and the need to center myself in the present, without forgetting always to inhale the spirit of Christ.

Hoping to reach Alda, the next day I began with a very muddy uphill path. A detour to try to avoid the mud led me, in reality, back where we had started. Sometimes life, whether a pretty road or a muddy path, has to be faced head on and taken as it comes, without looking for detours. At the end of the day, it is not a big deal to get into the mud, since I can always get out and clean my boots. The climb was rewarded with an impressive view of the low plain and the upper part of the forest, with its lovely spring green.

Disorder

We left the city of Laguardia on a gorgeous, sunny morning headed for Navarrete, in La Rioja. Looking back, I marveled contemplating the magnificent scene of thick clouds that descended from the Cantabrian range, from which I had come the day before. I seemed to identify with that image: the route already traversed; my past, my regrets, and the disorder in my life. The meditation continued over the Ebro river, the towns of Lapuebla de Labarca and Fuenmayor, until I felt completely moved by the inner spiritual atmosphere of the Basilica of Santa María, in Navarrete. I could only kneel down and praise our Lady's presence before the overwhelming golden altarpiece, replete with biblical figures. With the background music, following a serene clarinet, I abandoned all my reservations and sincerely asked forgiveness. Sin, my disordered tendencies, the abusive insistence on satisfying my own need for security, money, comfort . . . My eyes teared up with shame, sincere laments, and hopeful gratitude.

Save the Muslim, leave the friend behind, and take two stones to Montserrat

In Luceni, God saved the Muslim traveler from the ire of Ignatius, but he also saved Ignatius from committing an act that could have had grave consequences. To leave a decision in the hands of a mule does not exactly explain the value of discernment. I reflected on how many times I had left the ultimate decision up to circumstances instead of to God.

Days later, in the train station in Zaragoza, I experienced the sadness of seeing our pilgrim friend Michael obliged to abandon the Way because of personal circumstances. I deeply felt the weight of uncertainty in life and in personal relationships. My faith returned after visiting the Basilica del Pilar. The Pillar symbolizes the Presence. But even when the Pillar is not there, the Lord is always present. I remember a very tranquil dinner together, pilgrims of life.

The next day the way was full of small stones and pebbles, very likely from the Ebro, that were almost surely the cause of my blisters. I observed that very few of the pebbles were perfect. People are also like that. I took two small stones from the path: one for my wounds, the wounds of life and of love; the other for the wounds of my loved one. I decided to carry them with me and walk with them to Montserrat, where I wished to offer them to the *Moreneta*, just as Ignatius had offered his sword. The way turned dry, and the atmosphere warm. Sometimes life is like that desert way. Keep walking, keep living, because Christ is with you.

When we pause, life catches up with us

I like the walk from Pina de Ebro to Venta de Santa Lucia, for the most part through the desert of fields that do not flower sufficiently under the implacable sun. I like this stretch, since it is very tranquil and suitable for meditation. We did not run into a single soul, except, there in the distance, the speeding pickup of some local farmer. No other vehicle, since we were far from the main highways. I walked with the pebbles in my backpack, thinking deeply of the wounds of the past. There were many moments when I felt the temptation to change and to choose other stones that seemed better to me; but I decided to leave off this search, which distracted me, and to walk with my head up, appreciating the desert and the empty shepherds' refuges next to the road. It was a full day in the desert, an experience of tranquility, aridity, and heat. The ground was sterile, and practically nothing could be cultivated, although the very life of nature still nurtured some lovely flowers. I wrote in my diary: "When we pause, life catches up with us."

Prayer in the desert

The desert is disencumberment and commitment. Who am I? Am I my possessions or my reputation? Do I form part of the beloved creation of God? Why am I important? Is it because others know me or because God has chosen me? I feel that Jesus is inviting me to lighten my load. He wants me to be able to follow him in freedom. Although I thought that I had put far fewer things in my backpack for this trip, now I discover that I could have permitted myself the luxury of doing without at least half of them. That is how life is.

I begin my prayer in the desert for my dear ones: "Lord Jesus, please accept my following you. You are the only one who can heal us. You granted the Holy Blessing to the people I love. On our way together, we learned and we grew, we stumbled and we got up, and we stumbled once again. These last thirty years have not turned out to be an easy road, but through your goodness and your grace, Lord, I can say that we now walk behind you. Please, accept this following and create the union necessary to serve your desire and greater glory. Oh Lord, hide me in your wounds."

The lessons of the blisters on the feet

My experience is that they must be treated rapidly. Never delay or look the other way. Ignoring them is not going to help and will only manage to make them worse. To suffer and endure them is not a solution, either. The pain continues until it becomes unbearable and starts to affect the normal functions of life. Prick and drain the blisters as they appear; the longer the wait, the longer the pain lasts and the bigger the wound. That is how life is. When the conflict that you wanted to avoid appears and develops, the pain starts: it has to be treated immediately. Trying to ignore it means worsening. After the cure, the weak skin becomes stronger and resists the pressure precisely at the very location of the pain. That is what I learn from pain: it is necessary to confront it, face it, receive it . . . , and thus life is strengthened in that area.

Reflections in Verdú

Verdú is the birthplace of the Catalan saint, Saint Peter Claver, who decided to leave his world never to come back to it and to dedicate his life to the service of the black slaves in Colombia. For us pilgrims, Verdú is a place of rest in the shelter prepared next to the sanctuary. Peter Claver made a decision in his life that changed him forever, and I felt anxious to make a decision about the unresolved crisis that had brought me to this pilgrimage: I felt that I had to take advantage of this experience, since I would never be able to come back to these places, either.

I felt that I received a message: this is a time of waiting and of personal transformation. Now is the right time to develop the inner virtues and to be guided by the Holy Spirit. It is necessary to continue growing in Christ and in his Kingdom. I had to accept the time necessary to go through the process and to be grateful for the moment of growth in which I find myself; to follow the model of Mary and the disciples just after the death of Jesus: in reality, they had nothing to do or to perform except to be attentive and willing to follow the will of God. Therefore, I understood that, instead of making a decision at that moment, I should be ready to make a decision precisely when God decided. It was an invitation to grow in serenity, to accept myself and my life; to accept the future just as it comes, with the inner peace in Christ. I was to cross the fog of my insecurity and try to find security in Jesus; to work on myself in order to be the man God wanted me to be; to become a healed man; to keep growing; to love God and love others.

Everything revolved around not making a decision at that moment but preparing myself to receive the necessary mental clarity when the right moment arrived; to take Jesus' hand and prepare to experience a growing serenity. Like Saint Ignatius, to let myself be led and not to decide before Manresa; to pause and let life catch up with me. Even in the worst situation, God is working. Faith is the strength for overcoming doubt. Faith is the wave of energy to overcome fear; which does not mean that fear does not exist. It is still there, but we jump over it.

"My dear God, I trust that you will do something to draw out the most positive. Even if I feel that I am dying, I know you are behind me. I know I am a sinner, but I am a sinner loved by you."

Offering the wounds

We began our ascent, on a foggy morning, from the town of Castellolí, to go up to Montserrat: the distinctive mountain range, the monastery, the basilica, the hymns of the Benedictine monks . . . and many tourists.

I went back three times to the chapel, very dimly lit, in a way that invites one to recollection, with the image of Christ in his crucifixion and an enormous image of Mary next to the dead Jesus. There I prayed with great fervor, reflecting on our wounds and pains, repenting my sins and asking forgiveness. Never before had I felt so intensely the Passion of Jesus crucified or the immense pain and the anguish of our Lady upon losing her only son. Tears and more tears in this sacred encounter. There I offered my own wounds to the

Virgin of Montserrat. I left the two stones that I had carried with me during the way.

At night, in the prayer vigil following Ignatius, praying the Way of the Cross, my profound inner awareness of Mary's pain and suffering was reinforced. My pain was not the same.

Liberation and gratitude

I walked thoughtfully toward the overlook of the Cross feeling a strange sensation of lightness of being: I was savoring an inner relief after the offering of my wounds. I enjoyed the quietude and tranquility of the surroundings, thankful that most of the tourists had already left, and I submerged myself in the lovely landscape of the sunset. The lateral erosions of the mountain looked like wounds in the rock, but they were beautifully harmonized with the overall natural landscape. On the path, a large statue of an angel also showed his wound, since he was missing an arm, but in the other he firmly held a sword. Wounds are a part of life. I choose to keep them until they are converted into sacred wounds, touched by God.

To my surprise, I ran into Father José on the return path. We chatted, and I thanked him sincerely for being our guide. In fact, he had acted as a spiritual-material director of the Way, both in the structure and in the essence of the *Spiritual Exercises*. He did the spiritual direction also through "works" and not only with "words". Through his direction I had deeply felt the value of the practical care, compassion, circumspection, and humility of the Ignatian Way.

Gratitude also to the people who have collaborated in marking the Way with those orange-colored arrows. There were arrows on solitary rocks, on borrowed signposts, or on walls of abandoned houses. These signs will remain there for years to give assurance and direction to future Ignatian pilgrims. I was moved to think of the goodwill of those who had painted those arrows in a desire to give direction and to create a new way for the experience of many in the future. That act means a lot in the serving and the following of Christ.

Reconciliation in Manresa

We left Montserrat under an intense rain and walking down-hill. I looked back several times to say "adios" to the lovely mountains and the holy place where I offered my wounds and my pain.

At last, we arrived at the destination of our pilgrimage: Manresa. The panoramic view from the nearby mountain was a perfect greeting to us from the town where Saint Ignatius reached his illumination and wrote the *Spiritual Exercises*.

I celebrated my belated sacramental reconciliation full of fervent repentance and like a poor mendicant begging intensely for God's forgiveness. God is an always merciful father who patiently awaits my return. When I repented and truly asked forgiveness, I was forgiven. I could not change the past or determine the future, but I could act rightly in my present and with the truth above all. I could be a new man to love and to serve.

I felt the energy of the hands in the reconciling blessing upon my head, and I experienced it in the sense that my Heavenly Father was granting his grace and his goodness to my whole being, body and soul. I returned to the chapel of La Cova, where the pilgrims had been waiting for me for a long time. My heart filled with peace and gratitude during the last Eucharist in La Cova, the end of this pilgrimage.

I do not know if my wounds are totally cured, but now I feel the pain in a very different way. I do not know if I am going to live and love freely and fully, but I am sure that I feel ready for it.

7

Pilgrimage as an Instrument of Personal Transformation and Growth

by Gillian McIlwain

This chronicle of my pilgrimage in May 2014 on the Ignatian Way has been an ongoing project since my return to Australia. It has taken on and changed its form on various occasions, and I have written some parts over and over again, adding things as time went by and the wealth and meaning of the pilgrimage became deeper and more stable. Now that I am obliged to finish my chronicle, I realize that my transformation still continues, that the healing is still going on, and that I am always going to be following in the footsteps of Saint Ignatius, knowing the love of Jesus and orienting my being and my tasks to the love and service of others.

This will be the final draft, written to help pilgrims and to encourage others by relating my experience, wishing to share the extraordinary spiritual experience that that Ignatian month in Spain represented and to confess that it continues to reverberate in my life, maturing, developing, and growing.

In reflecting about how I was going to describe my journey on the Ignatian Way, I found that the simple description of events could not really transmit what I had experienced. Therefore, I will also explain a bit of personal background.

An image has stayed with me since the pilgrimage, and it is what best lends itself to explaining the transformation, evolution, emergence, rebirth, and growth that I experienced in the Spanish natural surroundings through which we traveled. It helps to explain the change of nature on the outside, a change that in reality reflected my voyage of inner healing. It has to do with the growth and ripening of wheat. As a little girl, I lived on a farm in Australia, and I remember that my father took me walking through the ripening wheat fields, with the long stalks brushing my shoulders. My father used to stop and take a handful of ears and rub them between his large and sure hands, calloused by work. With these few ears, removing the grain, he showed me how to tell when the field was ripe and ready for harvest. He rubbed the ears between his hands, to and fro, and then opened his hands to reveal if the husks had fallen easily, thus leaving the ripe grain exposed. If it was exposed, then we knew that the small grain was ready for harvest and to be converted later into food or into the beginning of an endless cycle of life if the grain was resown in the soil to produce another crop.

Walking, I became aware of the abundant presence of wheat fields, which took me back to my infancy, applying in a simple way my knowledge of when it was time to harvest and to make hay and to get the best out of a wheat plant that, in reality, did not need human intervention for its transformation. The sun, the soil, and the rain, not man, had given rise to the ears of wheat. In its most simple and pure form, this is one of the grandeurs of God: creating for the sheer delight and amazement of seeing growth and transformation.

The small seed must grow along the Way

My journey along the Ignatian Way can be compared to the cultivation and the harvest of wheat, beginning with the fallow ground of my inner being. I desired to feel once again the presence of forgiveness and peace in my heart. The great number of daily events that reached me in the pilgrimage—the natural surroundings, the sounds, the silence, the smells, the breath, the crunching of the boots on the paths— everything acted as essential nutrients, so necessary for the growth and maturation of the plant. And just as the nutrients in the soil cannot be activated except in conjunction with the sun and the water that awaken the process of growth, likewise my thirst for Christ, thirst for understanding and forgiveness, compelled me to seek the calm water of the teachings of Saint Ignatius and the warmth of human companionship and love. And thus I realized that there, where the clouds of desolation and desperation loomed, dark indeed, heavy and threatening, a transformation of the threat into blessing came to pass with the silence and the walking. The clouds finally broke, but they poured out the life communicated by the refreshing water of the love and sacrifice of Christ, producing a nutritive inner cleansing.

This was my pilgrimage, which began with a small, shy seed put confidently into the hands of the Jesuits, who could put me deeply enough into the ground that I could take root anew, find God again after having walked so far away from him, and then, with the warmth and the grace of forgiveness, be converted into a plant that succeeds in growing strong to maturity, evolving, and being harvested, and then subsequently reinitiate the same process in an eternal cycle of communication of the life of Jesus.

Where to start, then? With this extraordinary pilgrimage,

which was at once unbearable, delightful, challenging, painful, desperate, liberating, enlightening, sad, desolate, enriching, peaceful, agitating, tumultuous, and occasionally chaotic, but on which I learned inevitably to open myself and accept the love and the forgiveness of God and to give love in return. I experienced the freedom that comes with the simplest of human knowledge, which is to feel loved, even in our insignificance, by the greatest of all forces and loves, which leads us to experience an incredible sense of intimidation and, at the same time, a great and pure liberation.

Abandoning oneself and trusting in God

I cannot explain, despite all my education in psychology, the feeling of profound inner satisfaction and peace that I have experienced each morning since I finished my pilgrimage. It was not a complicated or complex process. In the end, I was amazed by the pure simplicity of what I felt I had to do. Coming from my world, in which I am trained to present analyses and investigations, to criticize and to consider all the options, to develop the best strategies . . . , I realized that the only thing I had to do was . . . trust. Simply, hand over the control of my life to God and accept that, whatever happens, it will not be bad. And it turned out to be even better than that, better than good. What awaited me was a change in my life that freed me from the shackles that I knew I had; but, even more importantly, freed me from the shackles that I did not know were holding me captive.

I have spent more than thirty years trying to heal the deep psychological wounds of others, loving them and caring for them as best I could, but always avoiding the awareness of my own, in the belief that my wounds, my sins, were so terrible and unforgiveable that it was preferable to leave them be. Now I know that my search on the material journey along the Ignatian Way in Spain, far from my home in Australia, was in reality my way of discovering the face of God again, accompanied by the glory and magnificence of nature. I had grown up in the love of Jesus and had embraced him joyously since childhood and later as a young adolescent. However, a tragic event left me disoriented, as if thrown far from God, and then I felt far away from his reach and, indeed, from his gaze. In my eyes, I was unworthy, without any value, as is reflected in the words I perfectly recall having repeated in church: "I am not worthy to gather the crumbs that fall from the table."

After that terrible event in my life, I spent many years working hard to gather the sufficient personal courage to be able, at least marginally, to feel myself perhaps worthy to approach the shadow of God. But my successes were not enough, and, with the years, the wound inevitably weighed more and more on my poor heart; so I sought the consolation of a Jesuit retreat in silence, which took me to the Campion house in Australia and to the acquaintance of Saint Ignatius.

During the retreat, I felt attracted by the writings of Saint Ignatius. I steeped myself in the history of his life; I read all that I could about him—books, Google, articles—and in those pages I could see my own story: Ignatius, like I myself, did not feel worthy and had lived his life distancing himself from God's grace. I was tired and desired God in my life, but I had to find a way to get to the point that, when I saw myself, I did not tell myself I did not deserve him. Like Saint Ignatius, I knew I would feel better knowing God was someone close than I would feeling satisfaction with the woman who had constructed herself through her many achievements and recognitions.

And thus I began my journey, which, following a year of spiritual direction, culminated in my decision to undertake the Ignatian Way, a pilgrimage that, without my knowing it, would take me to the only place in which I had always remembered that God is found: the open space of nature, in the wheat fields, in the sky, in the mountains . . . and to doing what I had always done as a girl: walk and walk and walk and walk . . . through the fields of wheat growing for the harvest. I signed my commitment, I saved the necessary money, and I arranged everything in order to have the necessary time off from work (this, understandably, not without certain difficulties). I confess that at times I felt a certain apprehension and other ambivalent feelings and even fear of what I was going to encounter in Spain. Nevertheless, the life and the pilgrimage of Saint Ignatius and his process of discernment in life continued to attract me.

Synchrony on the Way, feeling the love of Jesus

I could write a treatise on my experience of the Ignatian Way in Spain. To explain what I felt when I got up each morning and opened myself up to the beauty of the Spanish countryside, to put on my boots and enter into contact with physical pain, to try to get my psyche functioning after a night of tormented dreams and tears, to give myself shots trying to reduce the pain and keep walking, to look out the window and enter into the peace of a serene dawn . . . And then to take one step, and another step, and another step, and another . . . The words to describe it would be as many as the steps I took, when I managed to find a rhythm in time with the crunch of my boots on the path, or when I felt the accompanying presence of another pilgrim fifty or more yards behind me, or the smile of Father Josep upon passing gently by me, always watchful and checking on my condition.

When walking, the body moves in synchrony with the air, and the waves that our matter creates in that air as it passes through it awaken. I liked to breathe the air at each step that my feet took . . . breathe, step . . . breathe, step . . . and I marveled at this incredible body that God had given me but that now demonstrated I had not duly cared for it. My amazement at myself grew as I walked and my body took me through the majesty of the Spanish mountains, the fields, the forests, the rain, the mud, the grass, and the streams. I felt blessed by everything: I could see, hear, smell, taste, contemplate beauty and feel myself in harmony with the world. And it is absolutely impossible to marvel at the majestic and the miniscule things of the world without becoming aware of the grandeur of our own corporality, head, and heart. And that, without doubt, is what happened on my pilgrimage.

Each day we worked progressively through the *Spiritual Exercises* of Saint Ignatius, always challenging and demanding in personal reflection and in contemplation. We celebrated the Eucharist every day at sundown, and with every change between the night and the next day another small change was taking shape. We exercised our bodies, which got stronger with each day's pilgrimage, but we equally "exercised" daily our souls and spirits, as we read, contemplated, or simply "felt" the word of God. We were transformed in many ways, some of which we did not perceive until the end of the pilgrimage, and even now, months after finishing the pilgrimage, some aspects are manifesting themselves for the first time.

As I have already said, many words would be necessary to describe my profound experiences of the Way; but two experiences in particular stand out and continue to live forcefully within me. They are mine, and they are very present to me.

The first has to do with the moment when I felt that I was a woman truly loved by Jesus. It was not a matter of a great epiphany or of a surprising discovery . . . Simply, this knowledge slipped into me very early one morning, while I was in bed looking at the morning sky through the glass window of a pilgrim shelter. The words of a children's song that I had learned as a girl in Sunday school and had almost completely forgotten came back to me in a clear, true, and edifying way after fifty-five years: "Jesus loves me, this I know, for the Bible tells me so. Little ones to him belong; they are weak, but he is strong." Where did these words come from after so many years? And they were so sweet, so consoling and reassuring, that, at that moment, I knew and felt deeply that he loved me, that he loved me completely . . . regardless of what I could have done or been in the past, and that all of the strength I needed was in the Lord. The day before, our route had taken us to visit the lovely church of Navarrete. There I had asked for forgiveness, as I had been doing along the way over the preceding days . . . and now here it was . . . in the simplest of forms and with great gentleness . . . in the forgotten children's song that had taken hold of my heart at a time in my life when Jesus was my friend, my companion throughout childhood, when I grew up jumping and laughing; a graced and marvelous childhood. Now, forgiveness and pure love; how blessed I felt . . . ! I got up in the morning in the pilgrims' shelter, far away from the fields I had run through as a girl on our farm in Australia, I put on the boots of a grown woman, and, without breakfast,

I took the little girl to the old stones of the street and put her feet again on the Ignatian Way to feel communion with the creation of God and with my newfound, rediscovered love.

It is probably worth the effort to point out here that the church of Navarrete was one of the most beautiful places of worship I have ever been in. From the moment we went inside, I felt the presence of our Lady. Although there were many marvelous and peaceful churches along the Ignatian Way, all of them places that provoked strong emotion, none was like this church of Navarrete.

Enduring the suffering that life brings us, but awaiting the God of Surprises on our way

Something else happened at that same moment. In the first days of the pilgrimage, I injured a knee going down the steep slope of Arantzazu, an injury that turned out to be very painful and that was getting worse. But I did not want to stop walking; I did not wish to lose the company of my fellow pilgrims, and I did not want to lose the marvelous union with nature that the pilgrimage on foot was offering me. Everything I had planned and wanted to do was not going to get away from me. I had everything established in my plans . . . Nevertheless, God had other plans for me . . . and with a surprise! Since I had to endure the physical and emotional drain that constant pain produces on pilgrimage, in reality I was being transformed into a person marked by compassion. It was a process of illumination in which my eyes and my heart opened to experiences I had lived many years before, such as living with my father, who suffered from serious cancer of the lower leg, which in due time would cause the amputation of his leg. A new understanding of the man who had shown me the simple way to know when to harvest ripe wheat, comprehending his daily battle with pain while continuing to be a loving father, made me experience great love and gratitude to his memory and for the life he had given me. Indeed, I had entered into a journey toward my past relationships and my physical, emotional, and spiritual wounds.

But God had not finished with my leg . . . He still had another surprise for me. Coming into Lleida, I could not walk anymore: the pain got the better of me, and I had to accept bowing out, traveling in a van, buying crutches, and learning how to get by with them. During this period, while I was recovering, I found myself with an entire day alone in silence, and that is when I had the second of my marvelous experiences.

Having started to get the hang of my crutches, I decided to get away from the van, walking along the path where my fellow pilgrims had to pass that same afternoon. I went off alone with my crutches. We were near Verdú, the town where the Jesuits have the house of Saint Peter Claver, and once again the wheat fields surrounded me with their beauty. I love the wheat farms in this part of Spain and the memories they evoked of my freedom running around our family farm. I decided to rest a little by the side of the road and to write something in my diary. I had dedicated a lot of time to contemplation and reflection along the way, but I had reserved little time for writing in my diary, so now I wished to take advantage of that moment of tranquility to write. But the God of Surprises was about to change things again . . . I found that I could not think of anything! Instead of writing, I caught myself looking toward the immensity of the wheat fields, wanting simply to walk

through them and lie down in their arms. So that is what I did! I walked carefully among the stalks that reached my hips, and I lay down on the ground with the ears swaying gently above me, like a frame around a picture, and I looked at the sky. In silence, and little by little, the reading of the spiritual exercise of the night before came to mind. It was about the crucifixion of Jesus on Calvary, his sacrifice, and the agony he suffered. I contemplated Jesus on the Cross, knowing that he died for me and what that really meant. What if that were what was happening at that moment of the way? The clarity of the moment was extraordinary. I became very aware of the wounds that Jesus suffered as a man. Wounds so painful and deep that they were unimaginable, and all so that I and others like me could see and believe that it was possible to live in sin, to feel desperation, and, yet, to know that we are forgiven and to live beyond those darknesses, in order to come to something more gratifying and marvelous. To feel that there was no end to life or to love. I was overtaken by a profound gratitude (and as I write these words, they do not seem sufficient to me) for what Jesus had done: his enormous act of love, the sacrifice of his life, accepting the betrayal of his friends and living the anguish of his mother —I comprehended also the sacrifice and the love of Mary offered to her son—made me feel the enormity of what had been done for me and what I had received, wretched as I was . . . ! And I loved Jesus for all of it. In fact, words of gratitude and appreciation came to me spontaneously, without needing to look for them in my mind: "I love you, Jesus."

In that incredibly simple moment, I felt overcome by the strong feeling of the presence of God, of his peace, meekness, and absolute satisfaction. I bathed in the sunlight in a wheat field, listening to the wind whispering through the ears. I had reencountered love, and now I could love thankfully and gratuitously in return. I stayed there without moving for two hours, in joyous simplicity, until I saw the vapor trail etched by an airplane through the sky. I took out my camera and slowly filmed the small world where I had nested in that moment, in the wheat field in a place in Spain where I found God again.

Still today, I often watch that little film. The images could be of any field anywhere in the world, in any country, just as God exists everywhere. For me, however, it was a concrete place that entered into my heart and remains there to this day.

Keep going, maintaining the rhythm

I left the field, again on the road awaiting the arrival of the pilgrims. I found myself walking with them for the first time with my crutches, carrying the weight of my injured knee, but without pain. I walked slowly at first and, then, with more confidence: the space inside of me to contemplate and to reflect had been reborn without the constant reminder of the sore knee. Although the crutches did not fit me perfectly, they allowed me to walk again with my fellow pilgrims and to continue on the Way of Saint Ignatius as I had desired. The crunch of my boots now joined the rhythmic sound of my crutches hitting the ground, and so I walked and walked and walked. My body moved anew through time and space, also mobilizing my inner journey. I am convinced that I would not have been able to experience the same sensation in the office of a physical therapist or in a church praying. In order to mobilize my inner self, I had to move and mobilize my body.

There were many other experiences along the Ignatian

"At this point of the pilgrimage, I know in my mind that God loves me just as I am, without my having to do anything to earn that love."

"Traversing the Ignatian Way on foot, I discovered how to put the brakes on life and to live day by day, step by step, making one single decision at a time, living in the present."

"The pilgrim walks with his past, which is cast in a new light."

"A phrase from Scripture sounded in my head: 'Whenever you enter a town and they receive you, eat what is set before you'."

"I have underlined in my diary the words of Jesus to Jairus: 'Do not fear, only believe. And then also a two-line fragment of a favorite song of mine: 'with love ... but just do not do it alone.' "

"My heart filled with peace and gratitude during the last Eucharist in La Cova, the end of this pilgrimage.... I do not know if I am going to live and love freely and fully, but I am sure that I feel ready for it."

"Finally, when the walking was joined with our inner voyage, the rhythm of the pilgrimage brought much peace, as we felt at each step the connection with the land and the opportunity to meld ourselves with nature, the sky, the trees, the birds ... and to see things from a new perspective."

The entire Ignatian Way is born from a wound: Ignatius of Loyola is defeated in Pamplona. But this turns out to be a boon for the future.

In his house of Loyola, convalescing, the Pilgrim is born, accompanied by the presence of the Virgin Mary.

"Thus appeared the phrase that describes the phase of the third week of my spiritual exercises: 'I am ready to do it'. That night I was willing to run the risk of sleeping in the desert, in unknown territory and under a new sky, in my solitude."

"Would I be able to walk the whole stretch? Or would my body give out on me again? When we started our march, I found myself saying to Jesus: 'I need you to be my companion on this stretch'."

"Everything I had planned and wanted to do was not going to get away from me. I had everything established in my plans ... Nevertheless, God had other plans for me."

"In that incredibly simple moment, I felt overcome by the strong feeling of the presence of God, of his peace, his meekness, and absolute satisfaction. I bathed in the sunlight in a wheat field, listening to the wind whispering through the ears."

"At that moment, I knew and felt deeply that he loved me, that he loved me completely ... regardless of what I could have done or been in the past, and that all of the strength I needed was in the Lord."

Monastery of Montserrat, site of Ignatius' reconciliation.

The plain of Los Monegros, where silence reigns.

The magic mountain of Montserrat, where mystery becomes experience.

Way, some of them very personal and distressing, others of great happiness and fun, and others related also to my professional life . . . Each one moved me in its own way to realize my inner way of transformation. As my wounds were exposed before God and were bathed in love and forgiveness, I had an ever greater degree of self-comprehension and knowledge. Some days I still felt overwhelmed by moments of confusion and anger, but each day I possessed a new and revitalized rhythm:

a. The pilgrimage in silence in the morning allowed me to put before myself the reflection and the prayer of the day; and as I walked and breathed, it matured within me, creating a space of knowledge and clarity.

b. Lunch brought with it the relief of rest and the company of my fellow pilgrims, the charm, the laughter, and the water . . . the lovely, reassuring water.

c. Later, in the afternoon, the last hours of the walk, the challenging fatigue, the growing desire to stop, together with the determination to continue on to reach the repose and the simple physical delight of a shower, with the feet freed from the boots and with clean clothes.

d. Then, at the end of the day, the sweetness of the Eucharist, where, despite each of us carrying our own personal progress, we shared and showed ourselves a true group of pilgrims, healing and reconciling the human antagonisms, coming to share freely our wounds.

Each day, our routine carried us farther toward our transformation as individuals and as a group. Our stories evolved to the degree that we continued to learn from one another, and we supported and offered love to our fellow pilgrims. Sometimes we felt very independent; at other moments, very close. But always together in the same direction every morning, praying together at the break of day and sharing the silence marked by the rhythm of our boots, our feet touching the path of Saint Ignatius and our eyes greeting the silence and the glory of God reflected in the majesty and the miracles of nature.

Going back home feeling the recovered freedom

By the time I got to Manresa, I felt exhausted, though physically, emotionally, and spiritually transformed. But it had been in Montserrat where the full realization of my change was most evident. In Montserrat I had the inner awareness that my spiritual and emotional wounds were healing well. I immersed myself in that marvelous mountain setting and could see the transformation that was taking place in my thoughts, reflected in my diary. I felt that the grain, held in the strong hand of God and separated from the husk after being rubbed, was ready for the harvest, to gather the benefits of my pilgrimage, to change my personal and professional life, to relate differently to others, to open myself to my family and to love, as Jesus did, and to walk as a pilgrim through life, giving myself to others as Jesus did on earth.

Truly, the Ignatian pilgrimage had been a way of healing toward freedom.

I returned to Australia, where the necessary surgical operation repaired my damaged knee, putting an end to the pain. But the transformation and the grace of God are still with me. At times, I still lose my way in life; at times I feel lonely; but I always know what is going to happen and that the trust and acceptance of God in my life are enough to be happy. I know that I am still following in the footsteps of Saint Ignatius, and I have no doubt that someday I will go back to Spain to walk again. My wounds have not totally healed, but the transformation of the healing experienced on the healing pilgrimage, that perfect combination of physical challenges and the silent company of the hand of God, has given me a peace and happiness that I have never before known. In my personal trust in God I found the necessary valor and courage to face my fears and know that I am free.

8

Pilgrimage as a Way of Initiation

by Alain Lemaire

I want to begin my account with certain personal information that might contextualize my experience on the Ignatian
Way. I am a French-speaking Canadian, and I made my pilgrimage at a time when there was no information in French
on the official website of the Ignatian Way. I wished to go
on a pilgrimage, and a coincidental reading led me to the
Ignatian Way. Since I did not have any experience of going
on pilgrimage by myself, I planned the stages of the Way
by printing the descriptions and maps from the website. I
thought—mistakenly, of course—that the proximity to the
French border would allow me to find easily bilingual Spanish citizens who could explain in more detail the routes to
follow. On April 21, 2012, I left Pamplona, alone and on
foot, headed for Manresa.

Ignatius says in his first instruction in the *Exercises* that he
understands a spiritual exercise to be "every method of examination of conscience, of meditation, of contemplation,
of vocal and mental prayer, and of other spiritual activity,
[. . .] methods of preparing and disposing the soul to free
itself of all inordinate attachments, and [. . .] of seeking and
discovering the Divine Will" (*SpEx*, p. 37). I also learned

from someone that spirituality is distancing from oneself in order to open oneself to others, and to the Other. Back home again, I consider my pilgrimage to have been a trip marked at once by cultural discovery, by prolonged and demanding physical activity, and by a time of profound and healing spiritual experience.

Walking with fear and reducing the view

For me the Way was, above all, a bodily and sensual experience. These elements rapidly became my companions, which helped me to be more aware of the present moment: the sensation of cold and heat, of wind on the skin, the hot water of the shower; the pain and the fatigue during the day of walking; the smells of the forest; the sound of the rain or of birdsong; the sunset over the mountains, the taste of coffee with milk, and so on.

I started out happy and lighthearted, but very soon I had to face my fears: those that I tried to hide from myself and those proper to ordinary life but that inevitably arose once I was on the road. For example, the fear of not being able to exercise any control over my life, which is normally very peaceful; from the first day, this fear appeared because I was not sure about the route to follow. I got lost every day because I did not plan my itinerary precisely, because I could not easily receive the aid of the people who amiably desired to help me but did not speak my language; and in addition, at that time, the signage on the Way was very limited. This part of the experience was painful for the first few days and prevented me from fully enjoying my physical surroundings and from feeling inner repose. In this sense, the French writer Philippe Nassif once said that as soon as we focus on a point on the horizon, we reduce our field of vision and deprive ourselves of the opportunity to perceive the essential, which many times is the unexpected. The more I fixed my attention on the importance of assuring that I was following the correct route, the less disposed I became to live and feel what was happening in me and my surroundings and to receive "the unexpected". After a few days, my fear began very gradually to subside. I better accepted the uncertainty and the miles that were sadly added daily to my pilgrimage every time I got lost. Upon entering into this new dynamic of acceptance, I began to receive the "miracles" of each day, small and great, which without doubt every pilgrim has experienced: an unexpected aid from a stranger, a lovely and magnificent landscape, or an inner spiritual revelation. Still today I keep this experience as a reference when fear of the unknown tries to overtake me again or when the events of daily life do not fall into place as I had foreseen.

Silence and the encounter with the other

The Way was also the occasion to live a long period of silence since, walking alone, I did not have the chance for long conversations with a traveling companion and neither did I connect to the web as I normally do. This inability to have long, drawn-out talks sharpened my attention to meetings with strangers: Valentina, the pleasant landlady of Zumárraga with whom I communicated only through gestures and short fragments of prayer; that farmer who offered me, in silence, a hunk of cheese and led me for a few miles toward San Román on the day I was soaked and freezing after a very long stage; Enrique, the priest and amiable innkeeper of the shelter in Jorba. After several encounters of this kind, this observation grew in me: in my life I also meet strangers with whom I spend a short time, or maybe years; but then life separates me from them, whether I like it or not. Who am I going to be for them in the time that we spend together? Will I be a benevolent person, or will I show myself to be indifferent?

Curiously, this experience of prolonged silence made me aware of the objective difficulties of truly listening to others, to the Other, and to oneself. When I meet someone or begin to pray, it is easy to introduce into the conversation my own worries or emotional states, thereby closing myself to what the other feels and experiences. After two weeks on the road, living more silently than a Carthusian monk, I met a traveler who spoke French and with whom I shared some miles of pilgrimage. At last I could talk to someone about what I had just experienced in the first half of my Way. Once we separated, I realized that I did not know much about him. I discovered that my words had been overly abundant and that I had lost a unique opportunity to listen to someone, a stranger, in a truly free way.

The initiate continues his pilgrimage in normal life

At the end of my pilgrimage, seeing what had happened in previous days as a type of reflection of my life, I said to myself: It has always been hard for me to delineate my path in life in a personal way without envying others, without fear of advancing, without grudges over the past, with security and flexibility, taking life as it comes, without a reference point on the horizon, and experiencing personal abandonment. By the circumstances that surrounded me, the Ignatian Way proved to be a way of initiation that committed me to follow the way of inner freedom and opening to life. In order to change, in order to convert, you have to accept the calls to dislodge yourself and get moving; and it is the inner movement that turns out to be most difficult, though it is the one that affords most life. Now I perceive Christ as the teacher of inner movements. When Jesus meets with Peter, with Zechariah, with the Samaritan woman, with Nicodemus, with Mary in her visit to the tomb . . . when Christ meets with Ignatius of Loyola and many others, is this not his invitation precisely to inner movement, to shaking up their ways of thinking that was keeping them internally blocked? Did they not open their lives and begin to receive Life in abundance upon entering into contact with him?

It has been almost three years since I set aside my backpack and life resumed its normal course. Nevertheless, rare is the day that I do not think about some experience from my pilgrimage and secretly feel the desire to be able to immerse myself again in the special "atmosphere" of that unique time of grace that is pilgrimage. Obviously, enough time has gone by since my return for the cloud upon which I floated at the end of the pilgrimage to dissipate. Now I realize that the more difficult pilgrimage is not the one that lasted thirty days on the roads of Spain, but the one that I continue to make, day by day, with the risk that habit and lack of attention might make me take routes that do not lead to a greater good, to the greater glory of God, as Saint Ignatius said.

9

A Way of Intercession

by Natalie Lacroix

During my pilgrimage in the footsteps of Ignatius, I had a profound spiritual experience, but not following the program outlined by the *Spiritual Exercises*. I remember my inner surprise when, at the end of my general confession at Montserrat, the Benedictine monk asked me how many miles I had walked. "423." "Good gracious, I would say you have already done your penance!" It surprised me, because I had not experienced a single moment of my pilgrimage as penance. I had not planned it that way. My motivation as a pilgrim was that of being able to intercede for all the people with whom I share my daily life. I recall, however, another pilgrimage following the footsteps of another holy Jesuit and companion of Ignatius, Peter Faber, in which I did experience the grace of conversion and healing that is documented in this book. But here what is discussed is the Ignatian Way, and so I enter into this Ignatian journey through Spanish lands.

She gives us her account of her pilgrimage even before the Ignatian Way as we know it today came into being. An abbreviated version can be found published in the magazine *Vie Chrétienne*: http://viechretienne.fr

Walking with others, with a hurt body

I admit that, as is said in the *Spiritual Exercises*, I have a "disordered affection" for Ignatius of Loyola . . . a story of privileged friendship that began at the early age of thirteen, at a time when I was the librarian of my class at school and, by chance, came across the autobiography of Ignatius, the story of a pilgrim whom I discovered to be a man with a heart of fire, in love with Jesus. From the time I read it, I became wild with desire to follow in his footsteps. Over the years, in my heart grew the dream to walk alone from Loyola to Manresa, in the style of the pilgrims of old, begging for food and shelter. In April 2007, I was diagnosed with a very serious illness that affected my lungs, and my first question to the pulmonologist was: "Will I be able to realize my dream?" The doctor's answer was affirmative: yes, if I did not go walking all over creation and if I had fellow pilgrims to make the pilgrimage with me and to carry my gear. Ignatius, his leg injured, hobbling and in pain, counted on his faithful mule; I had to count on the friendship of good companions.

Thus began an intense preparation, because, unlike that of Saint James, the Way of Saint Ignatius lacked tradition, and at that time I had to scout out the routes and consult the maps by myself, looking for places to lodge . . . I also searched out the most suitable equipment, in accordance with my circumstances, and began a specific training routine. I am a hospital nurse, and I needed a special leave of absence for all the time necessary to make the pilgrimage: not an easy thing, but which I obtained with the support of the whole team. Lastly, and most important, a group of Jesuits and members of the Communities of Christian Life offered to accompany me on the adventure.

August 13, 2010, was the big day. Étienne, a Jesuit companion, and I began our pilgrimage in pouring rain. That night, Marc, CCL, joined us in Zumárraga; a few days later, Jean-Benoit, another CCL, in Logroño; and others arrived later. From then on, we always walked in groups of four. The organizing was complicated since I was the only one who was walking the whole way, and the other three took turns.

Living the intercession for others in one's own flesh, in the footsteps of Ignatius

The purpose of our pilgrimage was to ask of the Lord great spiritual graces for the Community of Christian Life and for the Society of Jesus itself. The request was not that we do great works for the Lord, but that we dedicate ourselves to collaborating in his own works. This is probably what Ignatius invites us to ask in his *Spiritual Exercises* with the so-called "meditation on two standards": "to ask for a knowledge of the deceits of the evil chieftain and help to guard myself against them, and a knowledge of the true life which the supreme and true Leader reveals, and for the grace to imitate Him" (*SpEx*, p. 76). Likewise, to ask that we know how to show ourselves ready for all that God wants of us in every situation in daily life.

According to his autobiography, Ignatius decides in Loyola to perform great feats for God. He leaves on pilgrimage for Jerusalem, a long and dangerous journey, on which many lose their lives due to illness—hence the need for the famous hospitals along the pilgrimage routes—or to indigence. Ignatius wants to live a radical surrender to God through the practice of extreme penance, without seeking any kind of security for his life. It can be said that, behind this radical stance, in reality Ignatius served his own interests: he needed to restore his image wounded in the siege of Pamplona, if not for himself, at least perhaps in God's eyes . . . He still had a remnant of knightly pride.

His pilgrimage between Loyola and Manresa, his general confession, and, especially, the months of great inner trials in Manresa will purify him completely. As a result, Ignatius abandons those terrifying fasts which have damaged his future health, his interminable hours of prayer, his bodily austerity . . . to be led by God on a different path. And, little by little, Ignatius is going to consent to being placed where the Lord wants him to be in order to collaborate in his work.

This spiritual growth, which can appear to be linear, is in reality a constant struggle that develops with its ebb and flow in all of us. What interests am I serving? Am I following the path of good or of evil? Am I moving along the paths of the Lord?

Since our pilgrimage was one of intercession, we started each day by offering our current phase for a concrete team of the Community of Christian Life in Belgium and for a concrete community of Jesuits of the province, asking this grace for each and every one of them.

Prayer at the center

As a special privilege, since several of my companions were priests, we respectfully carried with us the Blessed Sacrament, and the person who carried it with him walked in silence all day, traveling at a slight distance from the rest and in a spirit of inner retreat. After two hours of walking, we paused for a reading in continuation of the Gospel of

Saint John. Then we shared our impressions and feelings and, following this brief exchange to help each other better understand the experience illuminated by the Gospel, we continued on our way in silence for another hour, meditating on the text. At night we celebrated the Eucharist in our small community, taking all the time necessary in order to experience the celebration deeply. In this encounter we had the opportunity to review what had occurred throughout the day. We took the time to recall the nudges of Providence throughout the day: all the guardian angels the Lord had sent us to show us the way, filling our water bottles, inviting us to stay with them, or suggesting that we seek lodging in the next town; the enriching meetings in which we shared the life of the Church and the harsh social reality that we observed on the way, like the hundreds of foreigners contracted to pick fruit, knowing their low wages; the exuberance of creation (the forests, the mountains, and the beauty of the fruit trees); and after rereading the Gospel passage meditated in the morning, sharing with the others the fruits of our prayer. This rereading of life allowed us to be aware that, as the Gospel of Luke says, our heart was inflamed during the time that we traveled as pilgrims on the paths.

On pilgrimage in poverty, giving thanks to God

The last point of this great Ignatian adventure that I would like to share is the experience of companionship. Paradoxically, I blessed the Lord for my illness. Without it, I would have struck out alone, in my desire to make a pilgrimage like Ignatius, and I do not think I would have made it to the end. Thanks to my companions, the pilgrimage was made possible and I would even say "easy", keeping in mind that we crossed the peninsula on a trip of 423 miles in thirty-one days and completely on foot. Some days we walked with temperatures of more than 104°F, through semi-desert regions.

An important dimension of the pilgrim reception that I would like to emphasize is, without doubt, the marvelous welcome and the affectionate attention we received along the way, especially in the religious communities (Poor Clares, Franciscans, and Jesuits).

Étienne had retained a reminder from his novice master regarding his own pilgrimage during his novitiate: "Pay attention, because during your pilgrimage the spirit of discord will also be your companion, looking to divide you." For this reason, walking as a group, we paid much attention to the quality of the relationships between us. It is very normal for there always to be one who has to make a huge effort to get up, another who has trouble closing his backpack and getting started, another who walks too fast, another who reads the map carelessly and gets us all lost . . . We paid attention to each other, learning to say things tactfully and at the right moment as tensions rose. This was even more important since we had decided to share our material goods fully, and it is well known that money ruins everything if the experience is not kept in context. It sounds funny, but I have to say that our level of detachment from things increased with the temperature: the hotter it got, the more things we left behind, in order to be able to carry more water bottles! But happiness never abandoned us.

We took very few things with us on pilgrimage, and, in this way, we found that with friendship, the Word, and the Eucharist we were able to surmount obstacles, go through many difficult moments, and end up profoundly happy.

There is no doubt that Ignatius and the six companions who took their religious vows together in Montmartre, Paris, on August 15, 1534, could give testimony to the same experience, they who also knew about walking long distances in company.

Yes, I have to thank my fellow pilgrims, who allowed me to realize the dream of my adolescence; and if God still gives me breath, I call upon them to travel together the last route of Ignatius: the Venice-Rome leg!

10

Living the Way of Life Calmly

by Terry Howard, S.J.

My Ignatian Way began in Pamplona from the same place where Ignatius fell wounded on May 20, 1521. I imagined myself carrying the wounded man back home on his stretcher. I would have liked to talk to him about his injuries, about the fight, and also to ask him if he was afraid of the uncertain future.

Next to Ignatius, getting over the wounds

I walked with Ignatius, burdened with "my wounds". To be sure, there were wounds at the beginning of my pilgrimage: I had asked for a year on sabbatical from my academic work; I felt tired, demoralized, suffering, and bleeding from past events and relationships. My wounds also needed treatment. Furthermore, my Jesuit provincial had recently asked me to consider a change to another job for which I felt hardly any attraction. I can still feel the tightness I had in my throat listening to his request! So that, like Ignatius, I found myself facing an uncertain future: possibly leaving my work and

142

people I loved, wondering if I would be free to respond to my provincial, wondering about how to make an important decision or, in fact, any decision that was properly united with God's wishes for me; and, at the root of it, wondering how to have a closer and more committed relationship with God. I thought over these kinds of "things" during my Ignatian Way, talking about them to Ignatius, to Jesus, and to Mary, taking the wounded man home and accompanying him farther. The trip from Pamplona to Loyola took me four days, going through Irurtzun (by way of Iza and Zuasti), Betelu, and Tolosa. It is a route of gorgeous landscapes, though with insufficient signage, but solitary and full of peace, which is exactly what I needed.

Upon my arrival at Loyola, I knocked symbolically with my fist on the great door of the house, as if saying: "Open the door! I brought Iñigo with me!" The next day, I went to pray in Ignatius' room, the place where he almost died from his wounds and where he lived during his recovery. There I took the time to write a letter that was very important to me: of reconciliation with a colleague to whom I owed an apology and wanted to offer my friendship. I wrote on small scraps of paper, which were all I had with me, choosing each word with care, paying attention to what my heart dictated. I had waited to find the peace of Ignatius' bedroom in order to write it. Afterward I sent it home by mail. With the issue back home thus concluded, a few days later I set out in the direction of Navarrete, with the converted Ignatius on my right and the Virgin Mary on my left. It was like finding myself in 1522. Except that now Ignatius would be seeing things through my eyes, not those of his time.

Lost and disoriented in the mountains

I stayed another day in Arantzazu to pray. I found myself in an impressive mountainous landscape, and, at midday, I went out to take a walk to see the monastery from higher up. I supposed that I knew where I was going, but I got lost in my thoughts and was paying little attention. After some time, I realized that I had gone too far, that in reality I was moving away from Arantzazu, and that now I would not be able to get back before nightfall. I thought it would be more secure to keep walking, thinking I would recognize some place I had passed by days before. The narrow mountain path was almost invisible beneath the fallen leaves. It was so easy to let my mind wander and to fail to pay attention to the path . . . ! Suddenly I realized: "I am in real danger!" My whole being went on maximum alert. "Stay on the path! Keep alert! Stay in the present moment! Do not let your mind wander!"

Embarrassingly, my "walk" took eight hours, fifteen miles, three bus rides, and a taxi. This experience made me reflect on the way I make my decisions, on what I do well and what I do not, and on my way of getting into trouble. I began to feel that the whole experience on the mountain was a kind of metaphor for my inner life. Perhaps I get lost too easily on my inner journey. Perhaps I let my work distract me, and I stray from the path of my "Inner Way" and stop walking with God. I began to ask myself: "How can I get off the path and let God fully be the center of my life?" I discovered a struggle between the desire to depend on myself and the desire to depend on God. Can I trust in God enough just to "let him act" and let myself be guided by him? I imagined Ignatius seeking a similar freedom.

Brotherly aid, humiliation, and generous reception

From Navarrete to Saragossa was twelve days of walking, with two rest days. The walk along the Ebro River was lovely: walking in solitude, accompanied by the sun, the silence, and nature. I remember the incredible pilgrims' shelter in Calahorra, the help and friendliness of the police in Calahorra, Alfaro, and Gallur, and of the Jesuits in Tudela. Whenever I had trouble or it seemed impossible to find a place to spend the night, the police always came to my rescue. Always!

To go from Saragossa to Manresa took me eleven days, with one rest day. In Fuentes de Ebro, two women from the town hall would not let me go on to Bujaraloz: "It is too long and dangerous", they told me. "It is practically a desert, and there are no places to lodge!" I let myself be guided by them, trusting that I was in good hands. So I took a train to the town of Caspe and, from there, the bus to Bujaraloz, where I enjoyed a more than memorable meal in the truckers' hostel.

In Fraga and Lleida they took me for a vagabond and treated me very badly in a shelter and in a restaurant. I can still feel the humiliation, the anger, my desire for justice, and my efforts to "defend my honor". Like Ignatius, I had wished to be poor with poor Jesus and to be humiliated with him; but when the experience came to me, I discovered that it was not easy to take. Only later, after calming down, was I able to find the courage and the wisdom of the experience. It taught me the way to be humble, to let go of my "wealth" (honors, recognitions . . .) and to be poor, as I had asked so many times in the *Spiritual Exercises*, following the same path as Jesus. I thought that Ignatius would have appreciated this experience.

From the beginning of my Ignatian Way, I faced daily the same question: Where am I going to stay tonight? And how do I decide? Should I let it be the budget that decides? I had made the decision to stay in simple places, the most economical possible, pursuing the ideal of the Christian pilgrim; but inside I would not take long to find a reason always to look for lodging with a bath: nothing better than a bath after a long walk! Every day the decision arrived, but without spiritual clarity about what was to be done.

Thus, leaving Lleida, I resolved to choose the poorest place to stay that night. In Castellnou de Seana there were only two options: the shelter or a bed and breakfast. When I got there, the shelter was closed. Mercy! I said to myself. I will have to go to the bed and breakfast where there is sure to be a bath. But the bed and breakfast turned out to be totally full. Now I did have a problem. I walked around town for quite a while, not knowing what to do. The owner of the bed and breakfast saw me and came up with her adolescent son, who spoke English. His friendliness and attention made me feel that he was really "there" in the situation I was going through, despite his young age. "Yes! The room is occupied, but they are leaving soon. If you want to spend the night here, I'll go clean it and have it ready for you in a couple of hours." In this brief encounter I simply felt welcome. A phrase from Scripture sounded in my head: "Whenever you enter a town and they receive you, eat what is set before you" (Lk 10:8). I immediately said yes! No sooner had I said it than, right at that moment, the manager of the pilgrims' shelter showed up. What confusion! What am I going to do? What is God saying to me? Is this a test to see if I am going to be true to my decision from the day before? I went to the shelter to take a look. It was cold, there was neither heat nor hot water, there were not any blankets, and I did not have a sleeping bag. I needed to sleep, and in such conditions I knew I would not sleep much that night in the shelter. So, I politely thanked the manager and declined the offer to sleep there. The truly decisive factor was the following: I felt I had to be loyal to the reception given to me by that teenager and his mother, a reception I did not want to deny simply for economic reasons. That would have been a mistake! "Eat what is set before you." I learned in Castellnou how to decide where to lodge: Stay where you feel welcome! Money need not be the main criterion. In the Kingdom of God, decisions are made, not on the basis of finances, but by the criteria of the heart. After that, I was attentive to the reception I received when it came to deciding on a place to stay. Clarity at last!

Going back home happy and stepping easy

After a few days I arrived at Manresa, exhausted and with thirty-three fewer pounds on my body. I showed up at the Jesuit community with no warning. I needed urgently to rest and eat, and my Jesuit companions generously offered me both things. A few days later, now having recovered some weight, I visited each place in the city associated with Ignatius, who was showing me his Manresa through my own eyes. It was an incredible situation to find myself in the hallway of a house and to know that Ignatius of Loyola had probably slept in that hallway or walked in that cloister. I left Manresa for Barcelona, and there were still agreeable encounters on the way: more people offering to help me just when I needed it. At the same time, a certain sadness also came over me, because I was coming to the end of my Ignatian Way and had to go back and live in the "comfortable world". And that did not please me at all! I had found something special and very important on the Ignatian Way, and I did not want to lose it again. "How am I going to continue being poor and making a pilgrimage like a poor dependent person in this world of abundance?" I asked myself. "How am I going to remain in contact with God?"

In Barcelona, I sat in the church of Santa María del Mar, in the same place where Ignatius had sat to beg. Perhaps the people who passed thought I was simply resting, or maybe even that I was a vagabond, too, taking shelter there from the midday heat. But on this point, Ignatius and I were one. I remained sitting there for hours, inwardly very content and in peace.

My pilgrimage from Loyola to Barcelona lasted thirty-four days: twenty-eight days walking and six days of rest. I walked around 478 miles. During those thirty-four days, I was able to process my life with Ignatius, Jesus, and Mary with the Holy Scripture and the *Spiritual Exercises*, applying the discernment of spirits according to the school of Ignatius. Many of the things that I carried inside of me I do not even remember now. For me the pilgrimage was a kind of "detoxification" of my life; much better than going to a therapist! In retrospect, God was putting me on my feet again and preparing me for the change in my life. Once back home, I was assigned to a new job and I said good-bye to the school, to the children, and to the city that had been my life for fourteen years. The Ignatian Way allowed me to find the spiritual freedom I needed to make this decision with God. Today I feel strengthened in my relationship with God, which I experience with renewed spirit. I feel that my wounds have healed! Convinced, I usually tell people that I have grown more in the last eight years than in the twenty-four preceding.

Traversing the Ignatian Way on foot, I discovered how to put the brakes on life and to live day by day, step by step, making one single decision at a time, living in the present. While I walked, I realized how worried and anxious it made me feel to think about what awaited me throughout the day. I said to myself: "This has got to stop!" So, deliberately, I have slowed my life down. I consciously refused to think about the future. And in so doing I discovered a new world of peace in the "step by step" of the trip; and that not only on the external way, but also in my inner journey. The result was that I felt much better about myself. And most important of all: by slowing down, I became very aware that I am walking in trust, counting on a benevolent "presence", and, thus, wanting to travel, maintain contact, consult, and make my decisions in harmony with the Spirit. It is very clear that the walking got easier when I did it in the presence of God.

Nevertheless, the benefits of making a pilgrimage on the Ignatian Way really appeared after my return home. Surprisingly, I found that the attitude I experienced along the Way stayed with me. I felt that I was still on the Way, only now in a different context and place. What I had learned then was being applied to the way I approached my work day, traveling the Way of daily life, you might say.

To this end, I walked to work and went home the same way, appreciating the walk and deliberately not thinking about the future or even about what I was going to do when I got there. This was my way of staying present to myself and keeping myself in the presence of God. I wanted—and this was my choice—to walk my life more slowly. I consciously rejected the "forcefully proactive" attitude, and I discovered myself to be less anxious and fearful. Life became more easily manageable. In an article titled "A Life without Hurry", by John Ortberg, my attention was caught by a phrase that sums up my experience on the Way: "You must ruthlessly eliminate the hurry in your life." "Hurry" is only another word for "living ahead of yourself, in the future, and, therefore, distracted from the Presence." The motivation underlying hurry is fear and not love; distrust and not trust, and it deceives us by leading us away from the right choice: that of trusting in the loving presence of God. The Way taught me to leave behind hurry, stress, fear, and anxiety, and to start to live a slower life in the present, in the peace of the Presence of God. I can say without doubt that today I am a happier person, thanks to Ignatius and to his Ignatian Way.

III

PRAYING THE IGNATIAN WAY: A DAILY GUIDE

by Chris Lowney

Spiritual Exercises for the Pilgrim

On occasion spirituality is defined as "the manner of transforming our journey through life into a way toward God". The following prayer guide, based on the *Spiritual Exercises* of Saint Ignatius, will transform, consequently, your physical, geographical journey into a spiritual one. Following the footsteps of Ignatius, you can also travel your own spiritual path, since these exercises were conceived largely during this phase of his life, a couple of them maybe even during the very pilgrimage from Loyola to Manresa.

Your pilgrimage is not only a journey *toward* God, but a journey *with* God, who is always beside us. Ignatius recommends that we talk to Jesus "as one friend talks to another", and the pilgrimage is an ideal opportunity to do this. The Gospels present us with Jesus and his companions in constant movement, traveling together from one town to another on foot, carrying their few belongings, exposed to the heat or the rain, just like you in the course of your pilgrimage. While it lasts, why not imagine yourself traveling in the company of Jesus and his disciples?

I hardly know how to pray; can I use these exercises?

Many of us are familiar with prayers already written, like the Our Father; but these "spiritual exercises" sound a bit sophisticated. Can "amateurs" do them as well?

Of course they can!

After all, Ignatius, when he started his pilgrimage, was also an amateur, lacking all spiritual formation; he had not even taken the equivalent of a high school religion class. He learned as he went, by trial and error, and he himself acknowledges that "God was dealing with him in the same way a schoolteacher deals with a child while instructing him" (*PJ*, p. 74). Trust in God! This is our most important advice for you in order to have a successful pilgrimage. God showed Ignatius the way, and he will also show you, no matter how inexperienced you are or how uncomfortable you feel praying.

Trust in God, and trust in the process. Physical exercise requires a certain time before it pays off, and the same happens in spiritual exercise. Just like physical exercise, spiritual exercise can also seem a bit boring at first. You can feel stupid or get the impression that you are wasting your time. Persevere. There is growth though you might not be able to see it, just as seeds grow underground before sprouting through the surface of the soil. Say this short prayer every day, *especially* when you feel that it is not true: "I know that you are with me today, Lord."

We are not going to cram this introduction to the spiritual guide to the Way full of a bunch of detailed instructions. God and you will discover the style of prayer that best suits you. Throughout the present prayer guide, we will present some "Ignatian advice for prayer". To begin with, here are three simple pieces of advice:

1. The spiritual "itinerary" is divided into daily stages, as is the physical pilgrimage. Do not choose what you most feel like in each moment, as if it were a menu in a restaurant. Carry out the spiritual pilgrimage in the order here proposed, because each day's exercise is based on that of

the day before. If you are to cover the entire geographical route, do the twenty-six daily exercises in order, one after the other. If you are only going to be on pilgrimage for six days, utilize the exercises of days 1 to 3 and 5 to 7. For a ten-day route, use the exercises of days 1 to 19 and conclude with that of day 27; and if you are to be on the route for thirteen days, in addition to the exercises of days 1 to 9, do these others: 18, 22, 26, and 27.

2. Find out at what time of day it is easiest for you to pray, and convert the prayer of that hour into a habit. Maybe you prefer to pray during the first hour of your walk every day. Or maybe it is better for you to take twenty minutes each morning, before setting off, to reflect on the theme and the biblical passage of the day, and then another twenty minutes in the afternoon, once you get your strength back, to see what ideas have resonated in the depth of your mind while you walked or pedaled. Do what works best for you.

3. Keep a diary. Jot down key ideas or images that catch your attention. Reread your diary every few days, and notice what patterns seem to be emerging: they could be indications of where God is trying to lead you through this experience.

But how, concretely, should I pray? What should I do during the time of prayer?

Always begin the time of prayer by gathering yourself and putting yourself in the holy presence of God. If you are carrying a music player, listening to some of your favorite spiritual music can put you in the right state of mind to pray. But then, turn off the device. Center yourself by dedicating one or two minutes to fixing your attention only on the natural rhythm of your breathing, the sound of your steps, or the songs of the birds around you. Pray the Our Father slowly to lead yourself into the prayerful encounter with God.

Then, read the prayer guide for the day. The texts corresponding to each day include: (1) the key theme of the day, *the "grace"*, that is, a gift or illumination that you hope to receive with God's help; (2) the *theme of prayer* for the day; and (3) a pertinent *biblical passage*. Read the material carefully, and ask God to open your heart so that you are able to hear what he wants to communicate to you. Again, slowly read the text of the Scripture: let each word sink in; repeat words or phrases that seem significant to you; pause in places where you experience peace or illumination.

The next step is to meditate on what you have read: What may God be trying to communicate to you through this passage of Scripture, and what are the prayerful thoughts that it incites in you?

And then?

Well, each person prays differently, and you will become the best expert in your own prayer. The best way to pray is, at the end of the day, the one most natural for you, the one that helps you to know God better, to know yourself better, to feel closer to God, to understand the direction that God is inviting you to give to your life. These exercises are concerned, not with learning factual information, but with deepening your relationship with God in Jesus. As long as you feel closer to God, to Jesus, and to the Holy Spirit, your prayer is working adequately. As long as you feel more faithful, more hopeful, and more charitable, your prayer will move in a suitable direction.

But, even when you do not feel any of this, *never* yield to the temptation to quit, because it is certain that God is working within you, regardless of whether you feel it or not. Be patient, and God's paths will become evident to you. Trust in the Lord.

Romanesque, Gothic, and Baroque?

A last note that can help you to pray in the different churches you are going to find along the Way: let the sacred art, which for centuries has helped men and women, pilgrims like you, help you to find God in the columns and images, in the dim Romanesque spaces, in the luminous Gothic windows, or in the majestic Baroque altarpieces.

The Romanesque churches, often built between the tenth and twelfth centuries, are characterized generally by their rounded arches, their heavy walls, and a simple floor plan with solid columns and small windows. This was a response, in part, to necessity, because only as the Gothic style was evolving from the twelfth to the sixteenth century did engineers and builders discover that pointed arches, rib vaulting, and flying buttresses enabled the construction of much taller and more stylized buildings. That is why the Gothic churches convey a sense of verticality, rising up on high pillars that seem too slim to support the weight of the edifice. The sensation of lightness is accentuated by the greater thinness of the walls and the abundance of windows ascending to the sky, set off by pointed arches. The interior of the church is frequently in the form of a cross, as there is a transverse aisle that crosses with the nave at the transept, or crossing.

The Baroque style arose in large part in the Italy of the seventeenth century and was nourished by Renaissance ideals. The churches tend to be profusely ornamented, with sculptures of angels, for example, arranged around the pulpits and flourishes. The Baroque style developed when the Protestant reform swept Europe and the Catholic clergy decided to shepherd their flock in a more protective way. The Baroque churches tended to be smaller (so that the faithful did not feel "lost" in the vast Gothic spaces), and the pulpits no longer remained hidden next to the distant main altar, but projected into the body of the church, so that the preachers could direct themselves more easily to the faithful (without microphones, of course). The paintings and sculptures frequently emphasized the sacraments, the triumphant saints, and other distinctive elements of Catholicism, in contrast to Protestantism.

What follows is the sequence of exercises for each day. *Buen Camino!*

Day 1: God Is with You

Today's grace: To feel grateful for the constant presence of God in your life.

God accompanies you throughout the journey of your entire life. In this day you will deepen your awareness of the permanent presence of God in your life, reflecting on your own "story of grace". Let your mind wander in a prayerful attitude through your biography, but not as if you were making a presentation of facts summarized for a job interview; rather, ask God to show you his constant presence in your life, and let your history unfold as if God himself were narrating the "photo album" of the key moments in your life: "Look, I was with you here . . . and here, too."

Recall decisive turning points of your biography that you now consider providential. Visualize the faces and the actions of the people who have contributed to forming you as you are as well as those others who have taken care of you, loved you, and instilled adequate discipline into you. These people have been and are God alive in your life.

Draw *always* from your daily experiences for prayer: for example, the theme of this first day is that God is with you throughout the entire journey of life; so then, as you walk, pedal, or drive today, imagine God right at your side. Tell God why you are doing this pilgrimage and what it is that you expect from it, and listen to his answer in your heart. The following psalm will help you to set the tone of the day.

Scriptural passage

> O Lord, you have searched me and known me!
> You know when I sit down and when I rise up;
>   you discern my thoughts from afar.
> You search out my path and my lying down,
>   and are acquainted with all my ways.
> Even before a word is on my tongue,
>   behold, O Lord, you know it altogether.
> You beset me behind and before,
>   and lay your hand upon me.
> Such knowledge is too wonderful for me;
>   it is high, I cannot attain it.
>
> Where shall I go from your Spirit?
>   Or where shall I flee from your presence?
> If I ascend to heaven, you are there!
>   If I make my bed in Sheol, you are there!
> If I take the wings of the morning
>   and dwell in the uttermost parts of the sea,
> even there your hand shall lead me,
>   and your right hand shall hold me.

If I say, "Let only darkness cover me,
   and the light about me be night,"
even the darkness is not dark to you,
   the night is bright as the day;
   for darkness is as light with you.

For you formed my inward parts,
   you knitted me together in my mother's womb.
I praise you, for I am wondrously made.
   Wonderful are your works! (Ps 139:1–14)

Day 2: You Are Still Loved

Today's grace: Accept your own humanity and comprehend that you are loved by God.

[*Advice for prayer:* remember to start each day's prayer session by recollecting yourself, placing yourself in God's presence by praying the Our Father, reading the grace that you hope to obtain from the day, and asking God to bless you with that grace.]

Dedicate another day to your story of grace. Recall again the people who came to mind during yesterday's prayer. Thank God that he has put them in your life. Imagine that, one by one, you meet them while you are walking today and that you thank them personally for what they have done for you. God has been and is alive in your life in innumerable ways, including through these people. Be grateful!

And God has been accompanying you the whole time, even in moments when you might have felt abandoned by him or unworthy of his nearness. Today review your "story of grace", remembering tribulations in that you have experienced the absence of God, decisions you wish you would have made differently or episodes you lament or in which you have felt unacceptable to God.

But you have *always* been and are acceptable to God, and what you are asking today in prayer is nothing other than to be able to believe that God is with you, accepts you, and loves you always, *even in those moments*. As Paul says, not "anything else in all creation, will be able separate us from the love of God in Christ Jesus our Lord" (Rom 8:39).

The graces you are asking for today are: gratitude, acceptance of yourself, and a profound feeling of being accepted by God. If you cannot believe this completely, then pray with the father of the boy with the mute spirit: "I believe; help my unbelief." This day is not for discovering each and every one of the twists and turns of your life; for the moment, it is enough that you seek the grace to accept yourself because you are accepted without reservation by God.

Scriptural passage

> And he said to his disciples, "Therefore I tell you, do not be anxious about your life, what you shall eat, nor about your body, what you shall put on. For life is more than food, and the body more than clothing. Consider the ravens: they neither sow nor reap, they have neither storehouse nor barn, and yet God feeds them. Of how much more value are you than the birds! And which of you by being anxious can add a cubit to his span of life? If then you are not able to do as small a thing as that, why are you anxious about the rest? Consider the lilies, how they grow; they neither toil nor spin; yet I tell you, even Solomon in all his glory was not clothed like one of these. But if God so clothes the grass which is alive in the field today and tomorrow is thrown into the oven, how much more will he clothe you, O men of little faith! And do not seek what you are to eat and what you are to drink, nor be of anxious mind. For all

the nations of the world seek these things; and your Father knows that you need them. Instead, seek his kingdom, and these things shall be yours as well." (Lk 12:22–31)

[*Advice for prayer:* utilize the experiences of each day to enrich your prayer! Today's Bible passage, for example, is about how God cares for even the birds and the flowers of the fields. So then, pay attention to the marvelous display of nature as you cover today's route, and realize that God conserves and gives life to everything.]

Day 3: Why Are We Here?

Today's grace: Better understanding your end as a person.

Where are you going? Today you have started your travel with a goal in mind. How lost and empty you would feel if you wandered around the fields with no objective at all, lacking all awareness of meaning, all defined direction . . . ! Likewise in life, we need to have a direction, to be aware of a purpose deeper than our professional career or our way of getting our sustenance.

For what purpose are we human beings on earth? Our ultimate destination is the "house of God", which is to enjoy eternal peace and happiness in God's company; or as Ignatius sets it out in the *Spiritual Exercises*: "to save our souls". Jesus has shown us the path to this happiness with the Father: to love our neighbor, to make the world more just and peaceful, to be compassionate, to help the needy, and to show gratitude to God for his marvelous creation, respecting the earth and all people. When we do this, we satisfy our end: "we praise, venerate, and serve God our Lord", as Ignatius says.

While you are praying, think of the people whom you admire because they have lived to fulfill stimulating and praiseworthy objectives. Why do you admire them? How would you describe the goals for which they live or have lived? On today's route, tell God, your companion, the purpose for which *you* wish to live; and, as always, listen to the answer he gives you. The scriptural passage that follows will help you to pray about the human purpose of your life.

Scriptural passage

> And one of the scribes came up and heard them disputing with one another, and seeing that he answered them well, asked him, "Which commandment is the first of all?" Jesus answered, "The first is, 'Hear, O Israel: The Lord our God, the Lord is one; and you shall love the Lord your God with all your heart, and with all your soul, and with all your mind, and with all your strength.' The second is this, 'You shall love your neighbor as yourself.' There is no other commandment greater than these." And the scribe said to him, "You are right, Teacher; you have truly said that he is one, and there is no other but he; and to love him with all the heart, and with all the understanding, and with all the strength, and to love one's neighbor as oneself, is much more than all whole burnt offerings and sacrifices." And when Jesus saw that he answered wisely, he said to him, "You are not far from the kingdom of God." And after that no one dared to ask him any question. (Mk 12:28-34)

[*Advice for prayer:* if you are on pilgrimage in the company of others, perhaps you would like to organize every afternoon—or every other afternoon—a "faith sharing" session in which each of you can share the graces and illuminations

that have come to you. Listen respectfully to how God acts
in each of your lives, and finish by praying in gratitude and
asking God for his continual blessings.]

Day 4: Being Liberated

*Today's grace: To ask for a proper relationship with all
creation and freedom with respect to all that might prevent
you from living your purpose thoroughly.*

You know the place where you want to arrive at the end
of today's travel; but you will never get there if you are led
astray by picturesque byways and end up losing your bearings or, worse yet, if you chain yourself to a tree before
leaving. Such absurdities will never happen to you on your
pilgrimage, but on occasion they do happen on a much more
important journey: your life. We are so enthralled by the
attractions of this life that we lose sight of our destination:
God. We are obsessed to such an extent with money, social
status, fun, physical appearance, social networks, sex, and a
comfortable life-style that the purpose of our lives starts to
revolve around ourselves and our desires. We are only free
to travel the Way toward God if we are free *from* all of the
unhealthy attachments that might hold us back.

Of course, we should enjoy the marvelous things of this
world—the gifts of God to mankind—but only with the
right perspective: we do not want to allow created things to
become more important for us than the God who created
them. We want to maintain healthy and balanced relationships with people, with money and possessions, so that we
are not enslaved by things or "use" people.

Today's grace consists, simply, in reflecting on these general ideas; during the coming days you will have the chance

to identify "slaveries" or "unhealthy attachments" that are perhaps preventing you from living your human end completely.

Scriptural passage

> For those who live according to the flesh set their minds on the things of the flesh, but those who live according to the Spirit set their minds on the things of the Spirit. To set the mind on the flesh is death, but to set the mind on the Spirit is life and peace. . . . So then, brethren, we are debtors, not to the flesh, to live according to the flesh—for if you live according to the flesh you will die, but if by the Spirit you put to death the deeds of the body you will live. For all who are led by the Spirit of God are sons of God. For you did not receive the spirit of slavery to fall back into fear, but you have received the spirit of sonship. When we cry, "Abba! Father!" (Rom 8:5–6, 12–15)

[*Advice for prayer:* the diary. Remember to write down the thoughts, feelings, and ideas that occur to you. The very act of writing all of this is an exercise in prayer, because it can help you to formulate whatever thoughts God is communicating to you. A question for you to reflect on in your diary: What have you learned about yourself over these first few days of your physical and spiritual journey?]

Day 5: There Is Sin in the World

Today's grace: To perceive the harmful effects of sin in the world.

God's plan is for a world full of peace, justice, and love, where all people live with dignity and develop their full human potential. But the contemporary world falls far short of this ideal. Plainly put, the world is marred by sin. At this very moment, somewhere in the world there are sellers who are cheating their clients, parents who are neglecting their children, and governments that are denying citizens their right to a good education or to freedom of worship.

Ask God to open your eyes to the reality of sin during today's travel: observe some of the small cruelties that human beings habitually inflict on each other.

Bring to mind the horrendous violence and systematic injustice that fills the news.

Reflect on the pain and the chaos brought about by sin; the suffering that sinful human beings cause others (or cause themselves).

Remember the theme of yesterday's prayer: when we sin, we use people or things in a disordered way that damages our relationship with creation and with God.

Creation is God's gift to us; our gratitude (or ingratitude!) is manifested in the use (or abuse) that we make of it.

Visualize Jesus on the Cross, and remember that he entered into history to repair our damaged relationship with God; Jesus himself suffered as a consequence of human sinfulness. Talk to this Jesus, and describe to him your pain and dismay at all the sins you have seen.

Scriptural passage

> "But they say, 'That is in vain! We will follow our own plans, and everyone will act according to the stubbornness of his evil heart.'
>
> "Therefore thus says the LORD:
> Ask among the nations,
>   who has heard the like of this?
> The virgin Israel
>   has done a very horrible thing.

Does the snow of Lebanon leave
  the crags of Sirion?
Do the mountain waters run dry,
  the cold flowing streams?
But my people have forgotten me,
  they burn incense to false gods;
they have stumbled in their ways,
  in the ancient roads,
and have gone into bypaths,
  not the highway,
making their land a horror,
  a thing to be hissed at for ever.
Every one who passes by it is horrified
  and shakes his head." (Jer 18:12–16).

Day 6: I Am a Sinner

Today's grace (in Ignatius' words): "That I may have a thorough knowledge of my sins and a feeling of abhorrence for them. That I may comprehend the disorder of my actions, so that detesting them I will amend my ways and put my life in order" (SpEx, p. 58).

Yesterday you contemplated the sinfulness *of the world*. Today you are invited to pray about a painful reality: *your own* sinfulness. You sin. Everyone in the world does, even the pope. And Ignatius did, too, like all the rest of the saints. Plead for the necessary courage to face yourself and to acknowledge your sinfulness, as well as the pain and the chaos you have caused yourself and others with your sinful behavior.

Your purpose in life is to come nearer and nearer to God; but, in sinning, you move away from him, as if you rejected his company with the aim of traveling the journey of your life alone, focused only on yourself, as if you were the god of your own life.

Ask for the grace to feel sorrow for damage that through sin you may have inflicted on your relationship with God and with others. We all have our own weaknesses and sinful habits (or standards of living) that are difficult for us to control: acknowledge them, and ask God to help you overcome them. Here is a description that Paul gives of the human condition: "I am carnal, sold under sin. I do not understand my own actions. For I do not do what I want, but I do the very thing I hate" (Rom 7:14–15).

But the love that God feels for you is not diminished. Ask to feel shame and confusion for your habitual sinfulness, but ask also to experience *wonder* before God's love, unbreakable in spite of everything. You are a "loved sinner". Listen to the invitation of Ignatius: "Imagine Christ our Lord before you, hanging upon the cross. Speak with Him of how, being the Creator He then became man, and how, possessing eternal life, He submitted to temporal death to die for our sins. Then I shall meditate upon myself and ask 'What have I done for Christ? What am I now doing for Christ? What ought I to do for Christ?' As I see Him in this condition, hanging upon the cross, I shall meditate on the thoughts that come to my mind" (*SpEx*, p. 56).

[*Ignatian advice for prayer:* "colloquy" is the fancy word by which Ignatius refers to a simple prayer technique, namely, to imagine yourself conversing directly with Jesus, "as a friend talks to a friend". Ignatius recommends the "colloquy" as a fruitful way to end each prayer session: tell Jesus what was on your mind while you were praying, what questions arose within you, and so on. The *Exercises* are conceived to deepen your relationship with Jesus, and the best way to deepen a relationship with a person is by talking to him and listening (in the heart) to what he has to say to us. Make the "colloquy" a regular part of your prayer sessions.]

Scriptural passage

> Early in the morning he came again to the temple; all the people came to him, and he sat down and taught them. The scribes and the Pharisees brought a woman who had been caught in adultery, and placing her in their midst they said to him, "Teacher, this woman has been caught in the act of adultery. Now in the law Moses commanded us to stone such. What do you say about her?" This they said to test him, that they might have some charge to bring against him. Jesus bent down and wrote with his finger on the ground. And as they continued to ask him, he stood up and said to them, "Let him who is without sin among you be the first to throw a stone at her." And once more he bent down and wrote with his finger on the ground. But when they heard it, they went away, one by one, beginning with the eldest, and Jesus was left alone with the woman standing before him. Jesus looked up and said to her, "Woman, where are they? Has no one condemned you?" She said, "No one, Lord." And Jesus said, "Neither do I condemn you; go, and do not sin again." (Jn 8:2–11)

Day 7: God Forgives

Today's grace: To be profoundly aware of divine mercy.

God is always merciful. The parable of the "prodigal son" illustrates the mercy that God wants to show you in your life. Recall now how insultingly the son treats the father, demanding his inheritance beforehand, as if to tell him: "Hey, Dad, even though you have had to work hard to make this money, you do not matter enough to me for me to stay here with you. Give me my cut so I can get out of here."

After squandering the money, the son returns fearfully home. The father, who has every right in the world to be resentful and implacable, *runs* to meet his son and embraces him.

With this parable, Jesus reveals to us what God is like. Do you believe it? Do you believe such mercy is possible? Imagine yourself as the protagonist of this parable while you walk today: think of the stupidly sinful things you have done, and then imagine God literally running down the road to welcome you, forgive you, and celebrate your return. Many people drag paralyzing guilt and bitterness around with them; but God, the generous and indulgent Father, frees us from such burdens. Yesterday you had the courage to confront your sinfulness, and you showed yourself contrite; ask today for the disposition to accept what God freely offers you: forgiveness and healing. As you are walking today, imagine God freeing you from the pack of guilt that you may be carrying on your back.

Ask also for the grace of a forgiving heart like God's, the generosity to free from guilt those who might have hurt you throughout the journey of your life.

Scriptural passage

"'I will arise and go to my father, and I will say to him, "Father, I have sinned against heaven and before you; I am no longer worthy to be called your son; treat me as one of your hired servants."' And he arose and came to his father. But while he was yet at a distance, his father saw him and had compassion, and ran and embraced him and kissed him. . . . The father said to his servants '. . . this my son was dead, and is alive again; he was lost, and is found.' And they began to make merry." (Lk 15:18–20, 22, 24)

[*Question for the diary:* What have you learned about God in the last few days? Are your reflections making your image of God change or mature; your idea of who he is?].

Day 8: Will You Walk with Me?

Today's grace: To feel yourself personally called to walk by Jesus' side as companion and collaborator.

Your growing awareness of the merciful love that God feels for you may be arousing within you the desire to respond to him, and today Jesus invites you to formulate that response. It is not by chance that, in the *Exercises* of Ignatius, this call to work shoulder to shoulder with Jesus is heard right after having prayed about one's own sinfulness. God calls you just as you are: he calls the weak and sinful person that you are, not the unattainably perfect person that you would like to be.

Here, in the words of Paul, is the guarantee that God gives you: "My grace is sufficient for you; for my power is made perfect in weakness" (2 Cor 12:9).

Try the following prayer exercise: imagine that Jesus approaches you during one of the breaks you take today to rest. You are tired, disheveled, perhaps even a bit weary of it; but Jesus sits down by your side anyway, and he asks you to follow on his path. Admit that, almost surely, frustrations, weariness, and fear will appear, but I promise you that he himself will bear all that he asks of you.

How does the conversation develop? What does Jesus say when he tells you of his hopes and plans to transform the world? How does he formulate the invitation that he extends to you to join him in his mission? Ignatius imagines Jesus saying: "Whoever wishes to come with Me must labor with Me, so that following Me in suffering, he may also follow Me in glory" (*SpEx*, p. 68). Focus today on the wonder of Jesus calling *you* to help him carry out his plan to struggle against evil in favor of a more just, peaceful, and loving world. Tomorrow you will concentrate on your answer to this call.

Scriptural passage

> After this he went out, and saw a tax collector, named Levi, sitting at the tax office; and he said to him, "Follow me." And he left everything, and rose and followed him. And Levi made him a great feast in his house; and there was a large company of tax collectors and others sitting at table with them. And the Pharisees and their scribes murmured against his disciples, saying, "Why do you eat and drink with tax collectors and sinners?" And Jesus answered them, "Those who are well have no need of a physician, but those who are sick; I have not come to call the righteous, but sinners to repentance." (Lk 5:27-32)

Day 9: Your Answer to Jesus' Call

Today's grace: To respond generously to God's call.

Today concentrate on your answer to God's invitation. He calls you to use your specific talents in the creation of a world that is just and full of love. Ignatius imagined that, after reflecting on the merit of Jesus and on his mission, "all persons who have judgment and reason will offer themselves completely for this work" (*SpEx*, p. 68). *Completely.*

Ask today for the grace to respond generously to God's call. Maybe you have feelings like these: "In the past few days, I have felt the love and fidelity of God. God's plan for mankind has given me strength and vigor: I want to participate in it."

In your prayer, after imagining Jesus' call to you to share in his mission, respond to this invitation with the thoughts that occur to you spontaneously, including the worries that may be weighing on you at this point of the pilgrimage of your life. It is true that you do not know where the call of God might lead you. You know the exact route of your pilgrimage through Spain, but you cannot fully foresee your path with Jesus any more than you can predict whom you will encounter at the end of today's travel; so then, the generous response to God's call implies trust in the permanent goodness of God. Do not think today of the "call" of God as if he were asking that you take up a specific profession, such as that of a social worker, lawyer, or priest. Rather, God calls you, simply, to be a just and caring person in whatever may be the concrete circumstances of your present and future life.

[*Ignatian advice for prayer:* a "grace" is something that we want but cannot obtain on our own. You can feel "graced" to respond generously today to God's call, but you may also feel doubtful, insecure, or even indifferent. In the "colloquy" with Jesus, always show your true self, your authentic thoughts; do not "fake" the pious sentiments you are "supposed" to feel. You can always be sure that God keeps working with you, just as you are and in the situation in which you find yourself.]

Scriptural passage

> "Fear not, little flock, for it is your Father's good pleasure to give you the kingdom. Sell your possessions, and give alms; provide yourselves with purses that do not grow old, with a treasure in the heavens that does not fail, where no thief approaches and no moth destroys. For where your treasure is, there will your heart be also." (Lk 12:32–34)

Day 10: God Makes Himself One of Us

Today's grace: To value God's extraordinary decision to become one of us in Jesus in order to redeem us when we had gone totally astray.

Today meditate on the decision whereby God, moved by love, deigned to become man in order to save us and show us the way. Nobody will ever fully understand the mystery of the Incarnation of God; the very idea can seem absurd or impossible. But today's imaginative prayer exercise, adapted from the *Spiritual Exercises*, helps you to contemplate this mystery.

Tell God what you observe during today's travel. Take note of the people you run across, young or old, happy or sad. Then take a broader perspective: think about the places on earth where mankind has lost its bearings as a result of war, cruelty, suffering, or injustice. Tell God what you see. Then imagine God, Father, Son, and Holy Spirit, looking at all of us from their celestial perspective and taking in the totality of happiness and suffering, good and evil that exist on the earth.

Imagine the Trinity discussing the state of our world and coming to the decision that Jesus would enter into human history to restore our broken relationship both with God and among ourselves, mankind.

Reproduced below is a fragment of the text in which Ignatius describes this process; with a prayerful attitude, imagine and develop the scenes that it sketches:

> First, I will see all the different people on the face of the earth, so varied in dress and in behavior. Some are white and others black; some at peace and others at war; some weeping and others laughing; some well and others sick; some being born and others dying, etc.
>
> Second, I will see and consider the Three Divine Persons seated on the royal throne of the Divine Majesty. They behold the entire face and extent of the earth and They behold all nations in such great blindness, dying, and going down into hell . . . I will also listen to what the Three Divine Persons are saying, that is, "Let us work the redemption of mankind." (*SpEx*, pp. 69–70)

Day 11: Walk with Mary

Today's grace: To appreciate the call that Mary receives and the answer she gives, and to implore identical generosity of spirit for yourself.

Mary was asked to believe the impossible: that she was to bring God into the world. Surely she felt worried and afraid: after all, it was not as if God had handed Mary a detailed program explaining everything that would happen in the future.

As an adolescent pregnant before entering into marriage, in a culture that considered this a real dishonor, she must have felt embarrassed and been the object of rumors. You, too, might on occasion feel perplexed and unsure in the face of God's call, not knowing where it is taking you; or maybe you feel "out of place" in living a Christian vocation in a secularized world that sometimes considers religion outdated, naïve, or the fruit of mere superstition. Spend time today with Mary. Imagine her daily life, her thoughts, and her prayers during the months of pregnancy.

With Mary in an advanced stage of pregnancy, she and Joseph had to travel from Nazareth to the birthplace of Jesus, Bethlehem, on a trip of some 119 miles. They were a type of pilgrim, just like you. Imagine yourself walking today with them, maybe forming part of a small group of people traveling to Bethlehem together in the interest of greater security on the road, subject to the same preoccupations as any traveler: Will we get lost? What will happen if one of us gets sick or if someone assaults us? Multiply these concerns by a thousand, because Mary is pregnant. Ask for the graces that were conceded to Mary for yourself: first, to believe the seemingly impossible good news that God is with us in Jesus; second, to say "yes" to what God asks of you, even when the way that opens up before you is vague and uncertain, as it also was for Mary; and third, to want to pray Mary's prayer: "Let it be to me according to your word."

Here is how Ignatius invites us to contemplate this scene:

> I will see our Lady and the angel who greets her . . . , as the angel fulfills his office as ambassador, and our Lady humbles herself and gives thanks to the Divine Majesty. I will then reflect to derive some profit from their words. . . . Review . . . how our Lady, almost nine months with child, set out

from Nazareth, seated on an ass, as may piously be believed, together with Joseph and a servant girl leading an ox. They are going to Bethlehem to pay the tribute that Caesar has imposed on the whole land. . . . See in my imagination the road from Nazareth to Bethlehem. I will consider its length and breadth, and whether it is level or winding through valleys and over hills. (*SpEx*, pp. 70–71)

[*Note. Today's prayer prepares you to contemplate the Nativity itself, which will be the object of meditation tomorrow.*]

[*Ignatian advice for prayer:* today and over the next few days, Ignatius invites you to "contemplate" scenes from the Gospels with the aid of a technique he calls "composition of place", a rather lofty-sounding expression that designates nothing more than the simple process of using the imagination to place yourself right in the middle of a scene; for example, in the Last Supper of Jesus, you should imagine yourself taking part in the supper and fill in the numerous gaps left by the sparse Gospel accounts: What else would the people who appear in the scene be saying? What do the people look like, and how are they dressed? Imagine yourself as another person in the scene. What do you do and feel and observe as the scene gradually unfolds? Does Jesus address you? What happens in your heart as the scene develops? Ignatius believed that, by putting ourselves into a Gospel scene with our imagination, we experience Jesus and his message in a very direct manner, which is one of the fundamental objectives of the *Exercises*. So then, today you can contemplate the scene in which Joseph and Mary travel from Nazareth to Bethlehem, where Jesus will later be born: walk beside them, shape the scene, imagine your conversation, and take note of your reactions.]

Day 12: Jesus Is Born

*Today's grace: To appreciate the miracle that
God is born among us in human form.*

The story of the Nativity has turned into something too
sterile and sure: we see some serene parents, cleanly dressed
and taking care of a healthy and angelic Jesus in a tidy manger.
But "get real" with the help of your pilgrim experience, and
feel solidarity with this family. As a pilgrim, you are beat
after the day's walk and uneasy because you do not know
if you will find lodging for the night, when at last you get
to the town where you are headed; so, you can imagine
yourself arriving in town together with Mary and Joseph,
who are more than exhausted after such an uncomfortable
journey. You find out that the only place to spend the night
is an unsanitary stable. How ashamed and worried Mary and
Joseph must feel, facing the prospect of bringing their son
into the world in such a dirty place, without relatives or
a midwife to help them . . . ! What does it say about the
message of Jesus that he came into the world in this stable,
not in a palace? And that he entered our world as a poor,
vulnerable baby?

Meditate on the absolute improbability of all this, and
implore the grace of great peace and consolation: if he per-
formed this miracle, God can also, without doubt, do great
things in your life. Here is how Ignatius invites us to contemplate the scene:

> The first point is to see the persons: our Lady and Saint
> Joseph, the servant girl, and the Child Jesus after his birth.
> I will become a poor, miserable, and unworthy slave, look-
> ing upon them, contemplating them, and ministering to
> their needs, as though I were present there. . . . The third

point is to observe and consider what they are doing, the journey and suffering which they undergo in order that our Lord might be born in extreme poverty, and after so many labors; after hunger and thirst, heat and cold, insults and injuries, He might die on the cross, and all this for me. (*SpEx*, p. 71)

Scriptural passage

And she gave birth to her first-born son and wrapped him in swaddling cloths, and laid him in a manger, because there was no place for them in the inn. And in that region there were shepherds out in the field, keeping watch over their flock by night. And an angel of the Lord appeared to them, and the glory of the Lord shone around them, and they were filled with fear. And the angel said to them, "Be not afraid; for behold, I bring you good news of a great joy which will come to all the people; for to you is born this day in the city of David a Savior, who is Christ the Lord. And this will be a sign for you: you will find a baby wrapped in swaddling cloths and lying in a manger." (Lk 2:7–12)

Day 13: How to Tell the Right Path from the Wrong Path

Today's grace: To desire to follow Jesus along his path and to have the ability to know when you are on the right path and when you are not.

Today's exercise enables you to discern whether you are on the right path or the wrong one in your walking with Jesus. Imagine yourself coming to a decisive fork in the road of your life: you choose the more attractive path; you acquire wealth, you become proud and win prestige; you are very satisfied with your life and all that you have achieved for yourself. Only after years and years traveling this road, as you pass by a sign—that reads: "the road of the world"—do you realize that your life is centered completely on yourself, which is just what you did not want. You have gone considerably astray without even noticing it, as if some enemy had seduced you with the lure of money, pride, or social status.

You turn around and find the way to get back to that first fork in the road, where it dawns on you that Jesus has been there the whole time patiently waiting for you. He motions for you to follow him on his path, which is so different: "the path of service to others", just the opposite of selfishness. The freeways are very well marked: one can see with no trouble where each road leads. But the pathways of life are not always so clearly indicated. It is easy to drift toward the "road of the world" without realizing it unless the warning signals are known: egocentricity, desire for wealth and social standing, excessive self-confidence. Recreate the prayer exercise just suggested: What "forks in the road" have you come across in your life? What temptations have attracted you to the wrong path? Possessions? Money? Social status?

On the road of the world, we are valuable only to the extent that we are able to get others to admire us or to consider us valuable. On the way of Jesus, we are important and valuable simply because God has created us and loves us.

Scriptural passage

There is great gain in godliness with contentment; for we brought nothing into the world, and we cannot take anything out of the world; but if we have food and clothing, with these we shall be content. But those who desire to be rich fall into temptation, into a snare, into many sense- less and hurtful desires that plunge men into ruin and de- struction. For the love of money is the root of all evils; it is through this craving that some have wandered away from the faith and pierced their hearts with many pangs. But as for you, man of God, shun all this; aim at righteous- ness, godliness, faith, love, steadfastness, gentleness. (1 Tim 6:6-11)

Day 14: Free Yourself to Follow Jesus

Today's grace: The freedom to respond fully to the call of Jesus.

Yesterday you stopped at a fork in the road and considered the difference between the way of Jesus and the way of the world. Today you will reflect on how some people wish to follow the way of Jesus but never fully decide on it.

Today try out the following prayer exercise: imagine that you see Jesus walking in front of you. You want to follow him, but first you have to fill a big wagon with all of your worldly "attachments", those things which make up your daily desires: your wardrobe, the bigger house you have al- ways wanted, all the people you have tried to impress, the web pages that you continually consult, all your money . . . Imagine yourself dragging this wagon along the road: Can you keep up with Jesus? Imagine now that you put aside the loaded wagon and you just walk behind the Nazarene.

The meaning of this exercise? Some people want to follow Jesus but never truly make the effort to do it, while others seem to think that they can have their cake and eat it, too, that is, that they can follow Jesus and continue, at the same time, clinging to all their worldly desires and obsessions. Tell me what you love and pursue, and I will tell you who you are: where you have your treasure, there also is your heart. Ignatius invites you to keep yourself spiritually free *from* excessive attachment to worldly treasures so that you can be free *to* follow the way of God. Or, to put it another way, the grace for today consists in being free enough to go wherever God guides you for the sake of your deepest happiness.

Scriptural passage

"No one can serve two masters; for either he will hate the one and love the other, or he will be devoted to the one and despise the other. You cannot serve God and mammon. . . .

"But seek first his kingdom and his righteousness, and all these things shall be yours as well.

"Therefore do not be anxious about tomorrow, for tomorrow will be anxious for itself. Let the day's own trouble be sufficient for the day." (Mt 6:24, 33–34)

Day 15: Jesus Begins His Ministry

Today's grace: For the next few days you are going to implore the same grace, namely, to know Jesus more deeply, to feel his love for you, and to respond to that love by closely following him in his mission.

When he was around thirty years old, Jesus left home to begin his public activity. The first thing he did was to travel some seventy-five miles from Nazareth to the spot on the banks of the Jordan where John baptized him. With a prayerful attitude, imagine what Jesus could have felt or seen that spurred him to begin his ministry at that moment and not at another. Imagine that by chance, just as he is setting out, you meet him and that the two of you, walking abreast, spend the day together. Of course, you talk about the weather and the landscape. But, what else? What does Jesus tell you about this new phase of his life? And what thoughts do you want to share with Jesus at this point of your own journey?

You decide to take a detour from the route you planned in order to follow Jesus when he heads toward the Jordan. (Along the Ignatian Way, you will often see the Ebro; let the river be incorporated into your prayer imagination. Today it can be the "Jordan"; and in the next stages, an ongoing reminder of baptism and vivifying water.) Observe how the immaculate Jesus chooses to begin his ministry: not with a speech or a miracle, but entering into solidarity with the sinners who receive from John the baptism of repentance. What does John say when he calls you to conversion, you and the rest of the multitude? The word "conversion" means, literally, something like "to turn around", and John is inviting you to give a new direction to your life at Jesus' side.

Scriptural passage

John the Baptist appeared in the wilderness, preaching a baptism of repentance for the forgiveness of sins. And there went out to him all the country of Judea, and all the people of Jerusalem; and they were baptized by him in the river Jordan, confessing their sins. . . . And he preached, saying, "After me comes he who is mightier than I, the thong of whose sandals I am not worthy to stoop down and untie. I have baptized you with water; but he will baptize you with the Holy Spirit."

In those days Jesus came from Nazareth of Galilee and was baptized by John in the Jordan. And when he came up out of the water, immediately he saw the heavens opened

and the Spirit descending upon him like a dove; and a voice
came from heaven, "You are my beloved Son; with you I
am well pleased." (Mk 1:4-5, 7-11)

Day 16: Jesus Is Tempted

*Today's grace: To know Jesus more deeply, to feel
the love he has for you, and to respond to that love
by closely following him in his mission.*

Today we focus on the tempted Jesus. The Gospel passage
tells us that Jesus was *led* to the desert by the Holy Spirit:
the experience of the "desert"—that is, solitude and even
difficulty and crisis—has something valuable to teach us.
Satan tempts Jesus to make sinful use of the good things of
the world. Bread is good and vivifying, but Satan tempts
Jesus to turn the stones into bread by means of a selfish
miracle. The question that this poses to us is: Will you use
your power, your talents, and your resources in a selfish,
self-centered way, or will you dedicate your life to serving
God in loving others?

In the desert, Jesus learns above all that salvation does not
come of itself, but comes from trusting in God, who will
not abandon him: "Man shall not live by bread alone, but
by every word that proceeds from the mouth of God" (Mt
4:4). Use your pilgrim experience to compare your life to
that of Jesus: on the way you get hungry, and on occasion
you even feel exhausted; you are going to cross the semi-
desert Monegros, which allows you to get an idea of the
fears that arise in the "desert experiences" of life. What are
you learning about yourself in the desert moments of your
pilgrimage? Tell Jesus about the fears and temptations you
experience in life. Ask him for the grace to trust in God
during such moments, as he did.

Scriptural passage

> Then Jesus was led up by the Spirit into the wilderness to
> be tempted by the devil. And he fasted forty days and forty
> nights, and afterward he was hungry. And the tempter came
> and said to him, "If you are the Son of God, command
> these stones to become loaves of bread." But he answered,
> "It is written,
>> 'Man shall not live by bread alone,
>> but by every word that proceeds from the
>>   mouth of God.'" (Mt 4:1–4)

Day 17: Jesus Invites You to Follow Him

*Today's grace: To know Jesus more deeply, to feel
the love that he has for you, and to respond to that
love by closely following him in his mission.*

Following his baptism, and after having been tempted, Jesus
begins his mission, and he invites you to join him on his
way. Imagine that you are one of the disciples in the Gospel
passage that follows. You have heard about Jesus, and you
know who he is, but you still do not know him; suddenly,
you catch sight of him walking in front of you, and, when
you reach him, he turns and says to you: "What is it that
you are looking for? Why were you so interested in catching
up with me?" How would you respond to Jesus' questions?
What is it that you are *looking for* in life? Once you have
answered, Jesus says to you: "Come and see. Follow me for
awhile; find out for yourself what my mission is and what
my values are."

Jesus turns out to be so convincing that the new disciples
gladly leave their past behind so as to undertake a new way,
although they cannot clearly see what the future will bring.

Ask to meet with this so persuasive Jesus and to experience the attraction of his call. Ignatius invites you to reflect on the kinds of people whom Jesus calls to form part of his team: "Other points are also to be considered: (1) The Apostles were uneducated men, from a low station of life. (2) The dignity to which they were so gently called . . ." (*SpEx*, p. 114).

Remember to refer to your daily experiences on the Way to enrich your prayer. Notice, for example, how, even in the brief Gospel passage that follows, Jesus and the rest always seem to be in motion and how the "following" of Jesus is the dominant metaphor: we "follow" Jesus by imitating his values and his way of treating others on the paths of our own life.

Scriptural passage

> The next day again John was standing with two of his dis-
> ciples; and he looked at Jesus as he walked, and said, "Be-
> hold, the Lamb of God!" The two disciples heard him say
> this, and they followed Jesus. Jesus turned, and saw them
> following, and said to them, "What do you seek?" And
> they said to him, "Rabbi" (which means Teacher), "where
> are you staying?" He said to them, "Come and see." They
> came and saw where he was staying; and they stayed with
> him that day, for it was about the tenth hour. One of the
> two who heard John speak, and followed him, was An-
> drew, Simon Peter's brother. He first found his brother
> Simon, and said to him, "We have found the Messiah"
> (which means Christ). . . . The next day Jesus decided to
> go to Galilee. And he found Philip and said to him, "Fol-
> low me." (Jn 1:35–41, 43)

[*Question for the diary:* this spiritual guide includes ideas like "vocation" (or call) and "to be invited to follow Jesus." What do these ideas mean to you? Do you get the feeling these days that you are being called or invited to new values, to new habits? To a new life-style? To a closer relationship with Jesus? To what else?]

Day 18: Jesus Explains His Life-Style

*Today's grace: To know Jesus more deeply, to feel
the love he has for you, and to respond to that love
by closely following him in his mission.*

Jesus wants you to help him transform the world. His plan of action is simple: we will be living examples of values like honor, humility, and charity; we will denounce the injustices that we see; and we will treat others with love and respect. He outlines and develops these values by means of miracles, parables, and preaching, mostly in the Sermon on the Mount. Imagine yourself walking beside Jesus; during one of our rest stops in a Spanish town, some of the locals, for the most part unemployed and poor, moved by curiosity, gather to listen to Jesus explain his "way", his view of how we should live and treat each other. Visualize Jesus' listeners, people like those you are seeing or chatting with today. Recreate the moment in your imaginative prayer: How does the scene unfold? How do you and the others react when Jesus speaks? What are you saying to each other; what do you say to Jesus at the end? During the next few days, pay attention to what Jesus says and does to learn more about his style, his priorities, and his values.

Scriptural passage

Seeing the crowds, he went up on the mountain, and when he sat down his disciples came to him. And he opened his mouth and taught them, saying:

"Blessed are the poor in spirit, for theirs is the kingdom of heaven.

"Blessed are those who mourn, for they shall be comforted.

"Blessed are the meek, for they shall inherit the earth.

"Blessed are those who hunger and thirst for righteousness, for they shall be satisfied.

"Blessed are the merciful, for they shall obtain mercy.

"Blessed are the pure in heart, for they shall see God.

"Blessed are the peacemakers, for they shall be called sons of God. . . ."

"You are the salt of the earth; but if salt has lost its taste, how shall its saltiness be restored? It is no longer good for anything except to be thrown out and trodden under foot by men.

"You are the light of the world. A city set on a hill cannot be hidden. Nor do men light a lamp and put it under a bushel, but on a stand, and it gives light to all in the house. Let your light so shine before men, that they may see your good works and give glory to your Father who is in heaven." (Mt 5:1–9, 13–16)

Day 19: Jesus Heals the Broken

Today's grace: To know Jesus more deeply, to feel the love he has for you, and to respond to that love by closely following him in his mission.

Jesus to the people. In town after town, Jesus cures bodies and puts broken relationships with God back together, forgiving sins. Jesus tells a paralyzed man to get up and walk, rubs mud on the eyes of a blind man, takes the hand of a young girl who has died . . . and they are all healed! See how compassionately Jesus deals with the people who suffer;

how willingly he approaches those whom others consider repugnant outcasts. Jesus heals people, and he invites you to do as much by being receptive to the suffering people whom you meet along the way of your life, showing solicitude for them. As you walk today's stage, take a good look at all those who seem to suffer or to be sick or ostracized or who for whatever other reason need an encounter of healing. Imagine that the Gospel account that follows takes place on the outskirts of one of the towns you are going through today. Involve yourself prayerfully in the episode. You can guide the blind man to his encounter with Jesus. Or you can be the blind man himself. Do you have any inner blindness or suffering that you would like to ask Jesus to cure?

Scriptural passage

> As he drew near to Jericho, a blind man was sitting by the roadside begging; and hearing a multitude going by, he inquired what this meant. They told him, "Jesus of Nazareth is passing by." And he cried, "Jesus, Son of David, have mercy on me!" And those who were in front rebuked him, telling him to be silent; but he cried out all the more, "Son of David, have mercy on me!" And Jesus stopped, and commanded him to be brought to him; and when he came near, he asked him, "What do you want me to do for you?" He said, "Lord, let me receive my sight." And Jesus said to him, "Receive your sight; your faith has made you well." And immediately he received his sight and followed him, glorifying God; and all the people, when they saw it, gave praise to God. (Lk 18:35−43)

Day 20: Jesus, the Living Water

*Today's grace: To know Jesus more deeply, to feel
the love he has for you, and to respond to that love
by closely following him in his mission.*

A tired and thirsty Jesus meets a Samaritan woman next to a well and asks her for water. *Water.* At times the Ignatian Way follows along the Ebro River, where the vivifying water flows abundantly; but the Way also crosses the Monegros, a semi-desert region in which water is scarce. Traveling this arid landscape, you can get an idea of how important water was for Jesus' listeners. Without water, we cannot live, and Jesus reveals himself to this woman as eternal water, as the well that never runs dry.

In the Gospel account that follows, you can identify with Jesus, because you are also on the road and occasionally you get tired and thirsty. Visualize yourself today walking with Jesus and his companions, and imagine with a prayerful attitude that the Gospel scene transpires in some place that you go by. Watch how the encounter with Jesus seems to transform the Samaritan woman, in a way analogous to the way a healing encounter with him transforms suffering people. Implore the grace to meet this same Jesus, the well of eternal life, the person able to transform you.

Scriptural passage

> Jacob's well was there, and so Jesus, wearied as he was with his journey, sat down beside the well. It was about the sixth hour. There came a woman of Samaria to draw water. Jesus said to her, "Give me a drink." For his disciples had gone away into the city to buy food. The Samaritan woman said to him, "How is it that you, a Jew, ask a drink

of me, a woman of Samaria?" For Jews have no dealings with Samaritans. Jesus answered her, "If you knew the gift of God, and who it is that is saying to you, 'Give me a drink,' you would have asked him and he would have given you living water." The woman said to him, "Sir, you have nothing to draw with, and the well is deep; where do you get that living water? Are you greater than our father Jacob, who gave us the well, and drank from it himself, and his sons, and his cattle?" Jesus said to her, "Every one who drinks of this water will thirst again, but whoever drinks of the water that I shall give him will never thirst; the water that I shall give him will become in him a spring of water welling up to eternal life." The woman said to him, "Sir, give me this water, that I may not thirst, nor come here to draw." (Jn 4:6–15)

[*Question for the diary:* What is it that most gets your attention these days in the message of Jesus or in his way of dealing with others? Is the image you had of Jesus changing in some way? In what sense?]

Day 21: Jesus Invites You to Follow Him

Today's grace: To know Jesus more deeply, to feel his love for you, and to respond to that love by closely following him in his mission.

Jesus and his followers travel from Caesarea Philippi to Jerusalem, a week's trip on foot and some ninety-three miles over dusty, rough roads. Jesus is aware that he is heading toward a climax; in fact, this trip will culminate in the Last Supper with his disciples, followed by his Passion and death. Although the disciples, carefully chosen by Jesus himself, have already been accompanying him for a long time—some of them up to three years—they still have not totally "gotten" his message. They argue about which of them will be the most important in the Kingdom of God, and Jesus is obliged to explain to them once more that in the Kingdom of God, leadership means service to others, not status and honor.

Imagine yourself on this long trek to Jerusalem at Jesus' side, at times walking in silence and admiring the landscape or recalling the most noteworthy moments experienced up to now on this journey shared with him, at times walking in step with him so that he can participate in your preoccupations or in the doubts that his message incites in you at this point of your trip together. What do you tell Jesus? What questions does Jesus want to ask you, or what does he want to tell you? Ask to be able to comprehend ever more clearly who Jesus is; ask to be able to perceive with growing keenness what his message means for you at this moment of your life.

Scriptural passage

> And they were on the road, going up to Jerusalem, and Jesus was walking ahead of them. . . . And Jesus called them to him and said to them, "You know that those who are supposed to rule over the Gentiles lord it over them, and their great men exercise authority over them. But it shall not be so among you; but whoever would be great among you must be your servant, and whoever would be first among you must be slave of all. For the Son of man also came not to be served but to serve, and to give his life as a ransom for many." (Mk 10:32, 42–45)

Day 22: The Last Supper

Today's grace: To feel near to Jesus during the
Last Supper and in the Eucharist.

In a scandalous gesture, Jesus reaffirms that leadership entails service: at the beginning of the Last Supper, he washes the dirty feet of his disciples, a servile task that was typically done by servants of more humble standing. Imagine Jesus bending down to take off your boots and wash your feet after the long day you have spent on the road. Peter tried to resist Jesus' gesture of humble service. How do you react? Let us let Ignatius answer: "After they had eaten the Paschal Lamb and supped, He washed their feet and gave His Most Holy Body and His Most Precious Blood to His disciples. . . . [I] visualize the persons at the supper, and reflecting within myself, . . . strive to gain some profit from them. . . . To listen to what they say. . . . To observe what they are doing" (*SpEx*, p. 91). In prayer, visualize yourself taking part in this supper, imagine the progression of the banquet and Jesus offering you the bread and wine. Reflect on the fact that in each Eucharist you renew your relationship with Jesus. Recall, as part of your "story of grace", important moments of your life that have been marked by the Mass, by the Eucharist.

Scriptural passages

> Now as they were eating, Jesus took bread, and blessed, and broke it, and gave it to the disciples and said, "Take, eat; this is my body." And he took a chalice, and when he had given thanks he gave it to them, saying, "Drink of it,

all of you; for this is my blood of the covenant, which is poured out for many for the forgiveness of sins. I tell you I shall not drink again of this fruit of the vine until that day when I drink it new with you in my Father's kingdom." (Mt 26:26–29)

When he had washed their feet, and taken his garments, and resumed his place, he said to them, "Do you know what I have done to you? You call me Teacher and Lord; and you are right, for so I am. If I then, your Lord and Teacher, have washed your feet, you also ought to wash one another's feet. For I have given you an example, that you also should do as I have done to you." (Jn 13:12–15)

[*Question for the diary:* How would you describe the mission of Jesus in your own words? And as for yourself, how would you formulate the awareness that you have of your mission in life?]

Day 23: The Agony of Jesus in the Garden; Jesus Betrayed and Abandoned

Today's grace: In the words of Ignatius, "grief with Christ suffering, a broken heart with Christ heartbroken, tears, and deep suffering because of the great suffering that Christ endured for me" (SpEx, p. 93).

After the Last Supper, Jesus feels tormented while he prays in the garden of Gethsemane and wishes to be able to avoid the suffering he will have to undergo. He is betrayed by Judas, a disciple chosen by him, a friend. Other friends and disciples abandon him. He is humiliated, scourged, and scorned in public. The mission of his life appears to have ended in failure and the most appalling ridicule. Nevertheless, though abandoned by his friends, Jesus remains faithful: to himself, to the Father, and, by extension, to all of us, especially in the moments of sorrow, pain, or insecurity that we go through ourselves. Ask today to experience solidarity with Christ and compassion for him. All human life entails a certain measure of humiliation, rejection, and suffering: accompany Jesus while he finds himself exposed to the most abysmal depths of such experience. Today's grace is to desire to love Jesus enough to accompany him during the painful moments, just as a father, a mother, or a good friend does not leave a loved one alone during the most difficult times. If during your pilgrimage you go through the semi-desert Monegros, the inhospitable landscape can intensify the feelings of emptiness and disorientation appropriate for this difficult day of prayer.

Scriptural passage

Then Jesus went with them to a place called Gethsemane, and he said to his disciples, "Sit here, while I go over there and pray." And taking with him Peter and the two sons of Zebedee, he began to be sorrowful and troubled. Then he said to them, "My soul is very sorrowful, even to death; remain here, and watch with me." And going a little farther he fell on his face and prayed, "My Father, if it be possible, let this chalice pass from me; nevertheless, not as I will, but as you will." And he came to the disciples and found them sleeping. . . . While he was still speaking, Judas came, one of the Twelve, and with him a great crowd with swords and clubs, from the chief priests and the elders of the people. Now the betrayer had given them a sign, saying, "The one I shall kiss is the man; seize him." . . . And they stripped him and put a scarlet robe upon him, and plaiting a crown of thorns they put it on his head, and put a reed in his right hand. And kneeling before him they mocked him, saying, "Hail, King of the Jews!" And they spat upon him, and took the reed and struck him on the head. And when they had mocked him, they stripped him of the robe, and put his own clothes on him, and led him away to crucify him. (Mt 26:36–40, 47–48; 27:28–31)

Day 24: Crucifixion and Death of Jesus

Today's grace: In the words of Ignatius, "grief with Christ suffering, a broken heart with Christ heartbroken, tears, and deep suffering because of the great suffering that Christ endured for me" (SpEx, p. 93).

Accompany Jesus as he hangs from the Cross between two criminals. Spend time also with his mother, who contemplates her son gasping for air and expiring. *We* know that this drama culminates in the Resurrection of Jesus, but Mary did not know it yet. As Ignatius says: "Consider . . . the desolation of our Lady, her great grief and weariness, also that of the disciples" (SpEx, p. 96). Imagine with a prayerful attitude how totally perplexed and disoriented Mary and the disciples must have felt during those hours: the Jesus with whom you have shared the path for so long is no longer there. Meditate upon Jesus' words on the Cross: "Father, forgive them; for they know not what they do" (Lk 23:34); or "Father, into your hands I commit my spirit!" (Lk 23:46). Or those spoken by the criminal crucified at his side who asks that he remember him: "Truly, I say to you, today you will be with me in Paradise" (Lk 23:43). As always when you pray, "pause in places where you find fruit", as Ignatius says: if a certain image, phrase, or word moves you or particularly catches your attention, stay with it to discover what graces it holds for you.

Scriptural passage

> Two others also, who were criminals, were led away to be
> put to death with him. And when they came to the place
> which is called The Skull, there they crucified him, and
> the criminals, one on the right and one on the left. And
> Jesus said, "Father, forgive them; for they know not what
> they do." And they cast lots to divide his garments. And
> the people stood by, watching; but the rulers scoffed at
> him, saying, "He saved others; let him save himself, if he
> is the Christ of God, his Chosen One!" The soldiers also
> mocked him. . . .
>
> It was now about the sixth hour, and there was darkness
> over the whole land until the ninth hour, while the sun's
> light failed; and the curtain of the temple was torn in two.
> Then Jesus, crying with a loud voice, said, "Father, into
> your hands I commit my spirit!" And having said this he
> breathed his last. (Lk 23:32–36, 44–46)

Day 25: Resurrection of Jesus

*Today's grace: To be filled with happiness and to savor the
promise of eternal life that, thanks to the sacrifice of Jesus,
awaits us as our destination.*

In one of the Gospel accounts, that of John, Mary Magda-
lene informs Peter and the beloved disciple that the sepul-
cher of Jesus is empty, and both disciples run just under a
mile to confirm it for themselves.

During today's pilgrimage, put yourself in the place of
Peter or of John rushing to the tomb: What goes through
your mind? What do you say to the other disciples? Jesus
was dead, and now he appears to be alive again. What feelings does this turn of events arouse in you? The Scripture
underlines that "with God all things are possible", and the

Resurrection is the supreme example of this: God has made Jesus pass from death to life, on account of which, without doubt, he can also transform you. Jesus lives and is at your side, although you are not able to perceive him or even to believe it.

When the confused and frightened women who followed Jesus arrive at the empty tomb, two angels say to them: "Why do you seek the living among the dead?" (Lk 24:5). This same message is directed to us, who on occasion cannot resolve to accept the good news in its entirety. Ignatius advises you to let the beauty of nature increase the joy of the Resurrection: "Take advantage of the light and the comforts of the season, for example, the refreshing breezes of spring and summer, and the warmth of the sun and of a fire in winter, in so far as the soul thinks or can presume that these things may help it to rejoice in its Creator and Redeemer" (*SpEx*, pp. 102–3). Allow the experiences that you have on the Way to enrich your prayer as well. Recall with gratitude lovely places and moving experiences that you have seen and lived in what you have completed of the Way, and let such memories lift your spirit; imagine how the presence of the risen Jesus would lift the spirits of his exhausted disciples.

Scriptural passage

> Now after the sabbath, toward the dawn of the first day of the week, Mary Magdalene and the other Mary went to see the tomb. And behold, there was a great earthquake; for an angel of the Lord descended from heaven and came and rolled back the stone, and sat upon it. His appearance was like lightning, and his clothing white as snow. And for fear of him the guards trembled and became like dead men. But the angel said to the women, "Do not be afraid; for I know that you seek Jesus who was crucified. He is not here; for he has risen, as he said. Come, see the place where he lay.

Then go quickly and tell his disciples that he has risen from
the dead, and behold, he is going before you to Galilee;
there you will see him. Behold, I have told you." So they
departed quickly from the tomb with fear and great joy,
and ran to tell his disciples. (Mt 28:1–8)

Day 26: The Road to Emmaus

*Today's grace: To be filled with joy and to savor the promise
of eternal life that, thanks to the sacrifice of Jesus, awaits you
as your destination.*

Today the risen Christ walks at your side. Luke presents
two disciples who are on their way to a village called Emmaus, two leagues away (that is, seven miles) from Jerusalem
(Lk 24:13–35). Suddenly, Jesus in person catches up with
them, though they do not recognize him in his new risen
state. To this traveling companion, at first unknown, they
speak of Jesus, "a prophet mighty in deed and word before
God and all the people", who has just been condemned to
death and crucified. The two disciples admit to being deeply
discouraged, because they "had hoped that he was the one
to redeem Israel", and also confused and dismayed by an
incredible story of angels who had appeared by the empty
tomb of Jesus, confirming that the Nazarene had come back
to life.

   Jesus, who still had not been recognized, says to these in-
credulous disciples: "O foolish men, and slow of heart to
believe all that the prophets have spoken!" And he explained
to them how the suffering of Jesus had fulfilled the revela-
tions of the Scripture concerning the Messiah.

   On arriving at Emmaus, the disciples invite Jesus to stop
in and share their supper: "So he went in to stay with them.
When he was at table with them, he took the bread and

blessed and broke it, and gave it to them. And their eyes were opened and they recognized him; and he vanished out of their sight. They said to each other, 'Did not our hearts burn within us while he talked to us on the road, while he opened to us the Scriptures?'" (Lk 24:29–32).

This Gospel passage is ideal prayer material for a pilgrim on the road. Imagine yourself walking next to this "stranger", letting him know what you do not understand. Now near the place where you are going to spend the night, you invite this wise stranger to stop and have supper there with you; and upon breaking the bread, you realize that it is Jesus. When you recreate this scene in your prayer, fill in the gaps that the evangelist leaves in the brief account: surely the disciples must have asked Jesus what it was that he experienced upon dying and what it feels like to be alive again and in the company of friends.

What other questions would you like to ask Jesus as you near the end of the Way? What final ideas does Jesus wish to emphasize in his conversation with you? Ask for the grace that your heart, like that of those disciples, might "burn" while you listen to Jesus' message.

[*Question for the diary:* Make an evaluation of the Jesus you have known throughout your pilgrimage: Who is this person? What is his cause? What does he ask of you?]

Day 27: A Contemplation for Attaining Love

Today's grace: To find God in all things, to perceive how the love of God acts unceasingly in the world, to desire to love as God loves.

The *Spiritual Exercises* conclude by inviting you to savor God's goodness in all of creation and, above all, in yourself, since you have been created in the image and likeness of God. Recall all of the beauty you have encountered in nature along the several hundred miles of the Ignatian Way, think of all the friendliness of which you have been the object throughout the route: all of this kindness and beauty is a gift from God, an effusion of divine love over the world. And the natural response in an affectionate relationship is to offer your own gifts in return. In affectionate relationships there is "reciprocity": when we receive a gift, we feel obligated to give something in return; and whenever we make an offering of a gift, we share something of ourselves. Implore the grace to have a generous spirit, to find God in all things, and to be moved to offer yourself and your gifts to God in response to the love he has shown you. This meditation is a marvelous close to your pilgrimage and an ideal point of departure for the rest of your life. *In the words of Ignatius:*

> Love consists in a mutual interchange by the two parties, that is to say, that the lover give to and share with the beloved all that he has or can attain, and that the beloved act toward the lover in like manner. Thus if he has knowledge, he shares it with the one who does not have it. In like manner they share honors, riches, and all things. . . .
>
> [By way of preamble to this meditation, I] ask for what I desire. Here it will be to ask for a deep knowledge of the many blessings I have received, that I may be filled with gratitude for them, and in all things love and serve the Divine Majesty.
>
> *The first point* is to call to mind the benefits that I have received from creation, redemption, and the particular gifts I have received. I will ponder with great affection how much God our Lord has done for me, and how many of His graces He has given me. I will likewise consider how much the same Lord wishes to give Himself to me in so far as He can, according to His divine decrees. I will then reflect within myself, and consider that I, for my part, with great reason

and justice, should offer and give to His Divine Majesty, all that I possess and myself with it, as one makes an offering with deep affection, saying:

> Take, O Lord, and receive all my liberty, my memory, my understanding, and my entire will, all that I have and possess. Thou hast given all to me, to Thee O Lord, I return it. All is Thine; dispose of it according to Thy will. Give me Thy love and Thy grace, for this is enough for me.

The second point is to consider how God dwells in His creatures: in the elements, giving them being; in the plants, giving them life; in the animals, giving them sensation; in men, giving them understanding. So He dwells in me, giving me being, life, sensation, and intelligence, and making a temple of me, since He created me to the likeness and image of His Divine Majesty. Then I will reflect upon myself in the manner stated in the first point. . . .

The *fourth point* is to consider how all blessings and gifts descend from above. My limited power, for example, comes from the supreme and infinite power from above. In like manner justice, goodness, pity, mercy, etc., descend from above just as the rays from the sun, the waters from the spring, etc. (*SpEx*, pp. 103–4)

[*Question for the diary:* Now that you are nearing the end of your physical and spiritual pilgrimage, what are the main lessons that you have learned about yourself and about God? In what aspects would you like to be a different person?]

Day 28: A Contemplation
on Love and Gratitude

*Today's grace: To find God in all things, to perceive
how God's love is always acting in the world, to desire
to love as God loves.*

Read yesterday's text again and make a second meditation
on these themes. Focus today on gratitude. Be grateful for
the fact that you have so much, incredibly much: talents,
positive life experiences during your "story of grace" on
this earth, people who have been the presence of God in
your life throughout the years, and, last but not least, the
blessing to have enjoyed the energy, health, time, and money
sufficient to carry through this pilgrimage. Implore the gift
of generosity; ask to be moved to offer your multiple gifts
back to God (putting them in the service of his people).

[*Question for the diary:* For what things do you feel thankful
(both things you have experienced during this pilgrimage
and things you have experienced up to now in your life)?
Have you made some personal resolution to put into effect
in your life after completing the Ignatian Way?]